Sally Grantham

D1569305

# Vivienne Colle's MAKE-IT-YOURSELF BOUTIQUE

## by VIVIENNE COLLE
## with Marjorie P. Katz

## Illustrations by Mary Suzuki

*Published by*
M. Evans and Company, Inc., New York
*and distributed in association with*
J. B. Lippincott Company,
Philadelphia and New York

*Inspired by and dedicated to Caroline,*
*for her future.*

# Contents

|   I | Chic is Where You Find It | 9 |
|  II | Fabric Care and Handling | 18 |
| III | Basic Styles and Variations | 47 |
|  IV | Transformations | 147 |
|   V | Gifts, Accessories and Bazaar Items | 194 |
|  VI | From Appliqué to Zippers: A How-to Glossary | 231 |
|     | Index | 251 |

# Chic is Where You Find It

Welcome to my boutique! Walk along Third Avenue, on New York's East Side, until you come to Sixty-sixth Street. Turn east and there, on the north side of the street, just a few steps from the corner, you will find my place, *Vivienne Designs*. You really can't miss it. Two white carved stone poodles guard the entrance, and the show windows are crammed with swinging styles and clever accessories.

For years and years, while waiting on customers and making exclusive designs for a well-known Madison Avenue art needlework shop, I had cherished the dream of going into business for myself. I wanted to design only garments that I liked, using the most exciting, unusual and luxurious fabrics, and giving the most personal attention to my selected customers. Finally, I was able to beg, borrow, and save enough money to start making my dream boutique come true.

Now I design for some of the most famous and elegant women in America: Rosalind Russell, Audrey Hepburn, Elizabeth Taylor, Jacqueline Kennedy, Joan Crawford. I design for less-well-known, but equally elegant, patrons also. All can well afford to pay about $300 for a skirt, over $900 for a suit or coat, $1500 for an evening ensemble. All of my customers come to me when they want something extra special.

My forte is working with unusual fabrics. Antique paisleys, Indian saris, Victorian cut velvets — these are the stuff to whet my imagination and set my fingers and brain spinning. As I handle a luxurious piece of cloth that might once have been a priestly robe, or caress a faded Oriental rug, my mind leaps ahead to the fashionable garment I can create.

My regular customers know this about me, and when they travel search out exciting and exotic materials for me to work with. Joan Crawford bought an embroidered padded silk in Hong Kong — yards and yards of it, which I made into an evening suit for her, with matching gloves and hat. When Mrs. Kennedy returned from her visit to India, I was asked to come to the White House to work with the magnificent saris she had acquired.

My customers unearth unusual materials here at home, too. Rosalind Russell brought me a bedspread, which became a flowing theater coat. Audrey Hepburn got a pair of elegant slacks out of a silk brocade piano shawl with velvet embroidery and long silk fringe. And when Elizabeth Taylor came in with a two hundred-year-old needlepoint sampler, it was set as a front panel into a skirt of orange raw silk, where its muted tones could be displayed to the best advantage.

When I first opened my little shop more than fifteen years ago, the word "boutique" wasn't even in my copy of Webster's dictionary. Now boutiques are all over town. But for me and my customers, mine is still the most special of them all.

The word, of course, is simply French for "shop." But it has come to mean a small store selling feminine fashions, highly personal in style and of fine quality. Everything in my shop, from earrings to tents and from pot holders to evening gowns, is my own design.

This book is a collection of some personal favorites among these designs. Anyone can make them, following my instructions. All are easy to cut, easy to sew, easy to care for, and easy to wear for years and years. Most are flowing, easy-fitting garments — skirts that sit comfortably low on the hips, dresses that skim or bypass the waist, coats that are full and tent shaped.

10

These designs are flexible, too. You will discover a blouse that becomes a dress, a dress that becomes a coat, skirts and jackets that go to any length to suit you. Every one of them can be done in any fabric, from terry toweling to silk shantung; any one can be dressed up or down according to the way you see and trim it. Several of them can be combined to make day, evening, and at-home costumes. All of them can, and should, be made many, many times over — they will take on new personalities every time.

Here also are designs for unusual accessories for yourself and for your home, and all of which are welcome gifts. Every one is practical, and many are whimsical — a piggy bank made from a plastic bleach bottle, a necklace to match a coat or a suit, sneakers appliquéd to match your favorite sportswear, a smart hat made from scraps of fabric. There are a multitude of ideas for dressing up things you already have, or might even be getting ready to discard: a sleepcoat from a man's shirt, a new coat from a worn one, or an evening bag from an old clutch.

You will also find all of my favorite "tricks." I believe in doing things the easy way. Never sew if you can glue; never put in a zipper if snaps will do. Don't press anything if you can possibly avoid it. I also believe in doing things the thrifty way. Why search for antique velvet when I can teach you how to "antique" the newest velvet you can find? Why lament that you cannot find cloth or accessories in a certain shade when it's so easy to dye things — even little things like zippers — in a bowl or basin? I depend on tiny bits of luxury to make major effects, and so I use lace instead of seam binding even on garments made from fabric purchased in the five-and-ten. If you make your clothes reversible, you will be able to wear them twice as often, and it is just as easy to do this as to put in linings. And I believe in saving *everything*.

I never throw anything away; I am always making something new from something old. I learned my lesson about throwing things away a few years ago. I had tossed a book of

11

large wool swatches out with a heap of trash in a frenzy of shop-cleaning. It was late and I was tired when I finally went up to my apartment, which is in the same remodeled brownstone as the shop. But I couldn't sleep: tossing and turning, I kept thinking of the soft pastel plaids in that swatch book. After several restless hours, at three o'clock in the morning I went downstairs to the garbage bin and rummaged around until I found my discarded fabric. As a penance, I forced myself to stay up the rest of the night designing a suit made up of the slightly and subtly varied blocks of soft warm cloth. I have never thrown anything away since, and the suit that resulted is one of my favorite outfits to this day.

It seems to me that I have been designing all my life. As a child I whiled away the tedious hours of convalescence following a long-drawn-out illness by tearing apart old dresses that the other children gave me and redesigning them for myself and my dolls. A few years later I worked in a custom dress shop during the Depression, supporting a younger brother and sister on my earnings. Barely more than a child myself, I was gratified to find customers waiting for me, and not for the older and wiser salesladies, because of the care and attention I gave to fitting them and the individual touches I was able to suggest.

Those years provided me with the on-the-job training that was to be, although I didn't know it at the time, my own private school of design. I learned, using my own eyes and wits, what is flattering and what is not. I learned about styles, sizes, shapes; about fabrics, trimmings, and construction. I learned to know the figures of my customers so thoroughly I could cut whole garments for them without making more than two or three measurements; so well that I could finish their clothes perfectly with only one check-up fitting. I could even recall their dimensions perfectly as much as a year later. And, even more important, I learned how to find out what was going on inside of a customer — what she really wanted to look like, how she really felt about herself.

When a new customer comes in for her first appointment I take extra time to engage her in conversation so that we can get to know each other. I am a compulsive talker, and a compulsive listener as well. And I somehow manage to learn what I want to know about the woman's taste, her way of life, and what she thinks her style is. Then I am able to guide her taste, suggesting colors, fabrics, designs, accessories, to what I think she should look like.

For, just as much as working with extraordinary materials, I like to work with the customer in mind. I design to make my ladies look a very special way. Sometimes it is the way they want to look. When I design for Joan Crawford, for instance, I am constantly aware of the theatrical impact of Miss Crawford's name and image; and my styles for her are inseparable from other aspects of her strikingly effective appearance — her walk, her bearing, her makeup, her voice. But with other customers I sometimes sense that my gowns and dresses are needed to bring a touch of dramatic flair to a quiet personality, and then I design with this in mind.

I believe that women look their best only when they look themselves; but that sometimes they need help to bring out their real selves. Some women are confident and secure, knowing how they want to look and what looks well on them. But too many women are not sure of themselves. They have not learned what their own "style" is. They are hesitant about the effect they want to make. They try, perhaps, to copy an inappropriate model, instead of attempting to see themselves as they really are and dressing accordingly. For these women I especially enjoy designing, because in my clothes they know they look their best, and they gain a new confidence in themselves, a confidence that leads to improvement in their taste and style. I try to teach them their total appearance should be thought of when they buy even a single garment or accessory; that they should think of their clothing almost as if it were a stage setting. Clothes create an instant effect. They introduce one to one's audience, just as a stage set projects the mood for and introduces a play.

It is my belief that every woman can look and feel her sophisticated best only when her outfits are put together with her own unique personality in mind. It is not necessary to have a New York couturier design for you in order to achieve this chic. All that is necessary, in fact, is to heed that old adage, "Know thyself." Train your eye to be just as objectively critical of your appearance as you are of that of others. Learn to sense from the "feel" of your clothes when they look right on you. Do not hesitate to go to stores and try on garments that are perhaps "way out," things that you might never dream of buying, just to get the feel of wearing something different, something unusual, something *avant garde*, high fashion, or extravagantly elegant. You will probably be amazed to find that some of these clothes look and feel sensational on you. You will also discover, if you can make your eye really objective, that some details don't do a thing for you. You may have been wearing short sleeves or high waists for years and years without giving it a thought, but suddenly you might discover that these are not the best lines for you. There are too many women who became convinced years ago that they could wear only shirtwaist-styled dresses, and they have been looking increasingly dowdy as new fashions came in all around them while they wasted precious shopping hours searching for a style that was becoming harder and harder to find. Have *you* tried this season's styles? That is the only way to discover which will work for you and which won't, and how to incorporate the best of them into your wardrobe plans.

Your wardrobe should include those styles of an earlier year that also do something for you. It is in a combination of both old and new — the best of each *for you* — that you will find

14

your own style, and be able to dress with a new sense of chic. Current fashions are important, and this year's "look," whatever it might be, cannot be ignored. But more important still is the individual look every woman can create for herself.

It is not necessary to spend a great deal of money to achieve this chic. There is no relationship between the actual cost of making a garment and the effect you can achieve. One of my customers was delighted with an elegant satin evening dress for which she had just signed a $1500 check. As she took a last look in the mirror before removing the gown, she turned to me and said, "But don't you think it needs a touch down here?" She pointed to a side pocket, low in the skirt seam. The dress was perfect, of course, as it was, but I wanted to encourage this woman's developing taste and give her confidence in her ideas. "I have it," I said. "This scarf of mine is just the thing."

Taking a bright silk square from around my neck, I draped it in the pocket. The customer was delighted. "Yes, that's what it needs. Tell me where you bought it so I can get the same one."

Should I tell her? I thought to myself. Should I tell her it came from Woolworth's and cost twenty-nine cents? No, I decided: I'll just leave her with that happy feeling. And so I said, "Keep this one."

"Oh, but I couldn't."

"Yes, you must," I insisted, and I quickly took the silk square, removed the little tag that might have divulged its lowly origin, and tenderly replaced and draped it on the $1500 gown. The customer just floated out of the store, so delighted was she with the elegant finishing touch.

Millions of women have discovered that by making their own clothes they can have personalized wardrobes, and not clothing that was designed with a faceless mass in mind. Now, using my instructions and designs, even the woman who has never before made her own clothes can become her own dress-

15

maker. It is not necessary to have a sewing machine (I don't like to use them — I like to feel the material between my fingers as I sew). It is not necessary to know how to follow a standard pattern. It is not necessary, really, to know any more than how to thread a needle. The rest I will explain as we go along.

I will teach you how to construct a garment the way I do, but how to use your own individuality in finishing it. No two skirts should look alike. Every woman should interact with her materials, with her mood and ideas of the moment, to produce a unique item. I want your imagination to take over; for we are about to embark on an adventure in creativity. Everything you make must be a work of art — and love.

I can hear you saying, "Well, I'll try it. But what if I make a mistake?"

"What if I make a mistake?" I have heard this phrase, expressing fear and inhibition, countless times. And I always have an answer.

"Every mistake is a new design," I reply confidently. I know it to be true: it happens to me all the time, and so I can say it with conviction. "When you think you have made a mistake, look again at your work. You'll see that you have really started on a new design."

One of my most successful styles began as a mistake. I cut several inches too much from the bottom of a sweater being remodeled. "Oh dear, whatever shall I do with it now?" I said to myself. And just then along came the idea that turned my mistake into a new design: style the sweater like an Eisenhower jacket, with the bottom fitting neatly about the waist, and the rest of the sweater blousing softly over it. It was sensational.

Good design is really timeless. I have been making tents for years and years — as nightgowns and peignoirs, day dresses and evening dresses, and even as coats and jumpers. I expect to be making tents long after the current vogue has been replaced by a new "in" fashion.

16

I don't expect every design in this book to appeal to every woman. But every woman will find several things that she will love to make and wear. These are some of my favorite styles, favorite because they are so flexible. I recently surprised myself with an example of this flexibility. Rummaging through a pile of things from several years back, I came across a full skirt made of a rich brown cut-velvet fabric. The material appealed to me just as much as it had the very first time I saw it, years ago in a remnant bin in an upholsterer's shop. As I fingered it, regretting its now unfashionable length and debating whether or not to shorten it, I had the inspiration to hold it up with its waistband at shoulder level. Looking in the mirror I saw, not a too-long skirt, but the very latest thing in discotheque dresses. The waist became the decolletage and the hemline that was too long for a skirt was now fashionably above my knees! Before an hour passed the conversion was complete — narrow velvet bands were added to make shoulder straps, and two tucks were let out of the waist so it would fit around as an underarm neckline.

I know my methods are unorthodox, as unorthodox as the materials I use. This is what makes my work exciting. In telling you all my tricks of dressmaking and design, I will free your imagination to be as creative for yourself as I am for my customers. Let your imagination loose. Develop a "free eye" and discover new sources for designs all around you.

So, welcome to my make-it-yourself boutique!

# Fabric Care
# and Handling

There is really no limit to the materials that can be turned into lovely or clever fashion. I never saw a fabric I couldn't use. Each piece suggests its own transformation; every swatch has a personality of its own.

Many of the fabrics in the cubbies at *Vivienne Designs* were found at auctions or thrift shops. Some are real treasures. I have old tapestries, faded furs, antique rugs, and pieces of fine embroidery.

But I am just as fascinated with the textures and patterns of inexpensive materials. A length of cotton in a newspaper print became a conversation-piece dress. Ten-cent washcloths turn into whimsical baby bibs; straw place mats become decorative panels on gay skirts. Even bed and table linens turn into far-out fashions when I get my hands on them. And I give just as much devoted attention to working with these as to much more luxurious finds.

There is no end to the list of materials with which you can be creative. It is not necessary to work with heirlooms. But finding a fabric that is unusual and unexpected for what you intend to do with it is always an important first step. One of my most successful designs was a summer sheath of mattress ticking, which I luxuriously lined with pastel silk. A favorite trick of mine is to use upholstery remnants. These pieces of brocade, cut velvet, and antique satin are leftovers, too small to hang at a window or cover a chair, but just right for making a highly original dress or coat. Smaller scraps find their way into my quick-and-easy patchwork, which gets put together with contemporary speed but has an elegant oldtime air about it.

*Finding Fabrics*

I spend a great deal of time searching for unusual fabrics in every price range. Remnants of all sorts are good buys. Most yard-goods stores and departments have at least one counter where these pieces, left over at the end of a bolt of cloth, are tagged at very low prices. Sometimes you will find enough for a blouse or a dress or a lining; sometimes you will find two or three pieces of the same kind, enough to make an outfit. This is a good way to pick up unusual fabrics at bargain prices. Upholstery stores and departments also frequently have remnant bins where you can browse. Prices are usually low enough so you can afford to stock up as you find things, whether you have an immediate project in mind or not. Fill a carton or dresser drawer with your growing collection. (Under-the-bed storage chests, cedar-lined "hope" chests, steamer trunks, rattan chests, and even hampers are good fabric-storage places, too.)

It is not as easy to find good trimmings — ribbons, laces, braid, ready-made appliqués and so on — at bargain prices. But many of these are inexpensive to begin with. I always buy unusually attractive ones as I come across them. A carton filled with odds and ends of trimmings is a surprisingly useful addition to your work corner — it always comes in handy at the last minute to provide just the right finishing touch. In New York there is one neighborhood where these things *can* be picked up at bargain prices — on Thirty-eighth and Thirty-ninth streets, west of Fifth Avenue. Here millinery-supply and trimming manufacturers have their offices and showrooms, many of them catering to retail as well as wholesale trade. In some of the street-level shops you can happily spend several hours, poking through bins of ribbons, looking over tables covered with buttons, fingering acres of sequins and beads and feathers and all sorts of odds and ends. I always come away with shopping bags full of discoveries.

Thrift shops are wonderful hiding places for good fabrics. Don't think of the dress on sale as something old that belonged to somebody else. Don't consider it as something you might possibly wear. You are purchasing the fabric, and the trimmings, if any, of which it is made. You might also discover such usable things as embroidered pillow covers, needlepoint samplers or chair seats, and old tablecloths.

You don't have to look far to find leftovers. Chances are your own wardrobe contains quite a few. Out-of-style garments whose fabrics are still too lovely to discard should be viewed, not as old clothes, but as sources of fabric that might be put to another use. The full skirt of a no-longer-worn dress can become an A-line dress or skirt, or perhaps a shell and a matching lining for a jacket. A coat might provide the basic ingredient for a skirt and matching jacket.

Perhaps you are lucky enough to have an heirloom fabric of your own — a piece of needlepoint, a crocheted bedspread, or the large squares of paisley or brocade that used to be draped over grand pianos. If so, use it! Many people keep such things hidden away, in attic or drawer, saved for "someday" when "I'll do something with it." Why not let "someday" be now? I just can't understand the attitude that treasures something but refuses to utilize it. After years of searching I have acquired dozens of paisley shawls. Stacked in cubbies in my shop, they are clearly visible through the show windows.

One day a dowager, dressed handsomely in a camel-colored cashmere coat, peered in. "I couldn't help noticing those paisleys," she said. "I have one just like that at home."

In her dumpy hat and sensible if expensive brown shoes,

she didn't look the type to go for my styling. Still, I thought, it's not too late to make her feel glamorous. "Bring it in," I encouraged her. "I'll make you a coat or a suit."

"Cut it up? Oh, I could never let you do that!" she exclaimed, and went on her way, leaving me to wonder why she had come in in the first place.

I have no patience for people with this attitude. If they owned some fine antique jewelry they'd surely get it cleaned and wear it proudly. Why then hide a length of fine antique fabric? There is nothing I like better than being invited by a customer to go along on an attic treasure hunt. As I work my way through a wonderful collection of hand-me-downs, my designer's eye keeps seeing the possibilities for contemporary uses for yesterday's treasures.

*Putting Old Fabrics Into New Condition*

Every worn fabric must be in good and clean condition before you begin to work with it. Even shopworn remnants should be given a professional dry cleaning; this is not, of course, necessary for remnants in good-as-new condition. Whether your antique fabric is already made up into a garment or a flat item such as a sampler or piano shawl, dry cleaning is the first step. Remove any trimmings that will not clean well — fur or old buttons, for instance. It is not necessary to remove fringe, lace, or ribbons. When in doubt about whether a given part of a garment will clean well or not, ask your cleaner. Ask him also to press the garment only as much as necessary: overpressing might stiffen or weaken the fabric. Unless they are very crumpled, it is better not to press flat items at all: just smooth them out by hand and fold carefully. Fabrics to be dry cleaned include silks, satins, taffetas, brocades, chiffons, and woven wools of all kinds. An automatic dry-cleaning service is suitable for old fabrics.

Some fabrics respond better to being washed gently by hand, in mild soapsuds and lukewarm water. Stretch them out flat on towels placed over a bed (or a table or the floor) until dry; out of the sun, of course. This treatment is effective with various types of feathers, including maribou and ostrich, as well as with some knitted and crocheted garments of wool yarn. When washing feathers give them a good shaking and then hang them up to dry. The outline of all knitted items should be sketched on paper before washing; they should be gently pulled into shape, held lightly with stainless steel pins if necessary, and left to dry slowly. I always wash my paisley shawls by hand, in the bathtub, and then have them pressed by a professional dry cleaner.

## If You Are Reclaiming Fabric

If your fabric is made up into a dress or other garment, or if you are working with a shawl or bedspread, you will have to get a flat length out of it. Remove fringe, lace, and other trimmings. Fringe that has been removed from piano shawls or anything else can be used as trimming on skirts; can be used to cover shell blouses (see Transformation #4 in Part IV); or the fringe can be unknotted and the resulting long strands used as embroidery thread. If they are kinky from being knotted, wash in warm sudsy water, rinse, and lay out in straight strands on a towel to dry.

Never discard any trimmings that you remove from an old garment. There is no telling when you may find a use for an odd button or a bit of lace. Even embroidered fragments can be used in patchwork or as appliqués.

Next, remove zippers, snaps, hooks and eyes. Open up the darts, tucks, and seams, cutting one thread at a time. Use sharp-pointed sewing scissors or, better yet, the gadget called a seam ripper. Never pull or tear a seam apart; never pull or tear any trimming from a garment. These old fabrics have been weakened by the passage of time: their fibers have lost strength. The thread holding together an eighty-year-old dress is often stronger than the cloth of which the dress is made. So use all the patience at your command, but never strength. •

22

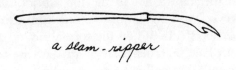

*a seam-ripper*

If the garment or other item is lined, try to keep the lining pieces together with the top fabric. The brocade piano shawls of several decades ago, for instance, consist of a layer of brocade on top of a liner, usually of cotton sateen. Sometimes, in the better shawls, a layer of padding is sandwiched between top and bottom. As the fringe is removed from around the shawl, use pins at the edges to hold the brocade to its lining layer(s). If you are reclaiming an old coat, pin the top fabric and its lining together as you free them.

When you have reclaimed flat pieces of fabric, press them gently, using a pressing cloth and steam. It is not necessary to iron on the wrong side if you use a pressing cloth.

### Bonding

Any fabric that is in a weakened condition must be strengthened before you will be able to work with it. Fabrics that are likely to ravel if cut into, such as laces or knits, must also be given support. The method in both cases is the same. The fragile material must be attached or *bonded* to a firm foundation fabric. Commercially bonded fabrics are now on the market: a knitted or loosely woven fabric such as a jersey is chemically attached to a backing that gives it extra body and support. You will use a needle and thread to bond your own fabrics.

The foundation fabric can be any cotton or synthetic lining fabric. Use lightweight foundations for lightweight fabrics; the heavier the fabric, the heavier the foundation needed. A knit or brocade, for example, might require a cotton sateen or even broadcloth foundation; a silk or lace might do well with a chambray.

The color of the foundation in most cases should match or

23

blend with the main color in the top fabric. On some occasions, however, you may want to use contrasting colors to achieve special effects. When the top fabric has an openwork design, as in lace or crochet, it might be wise to try several different foundation colors before deciding.

Always buy a little more foundation fabric than you think you will need. Sooner or later you will be glad to have it.

Work on a level, smooth surface such as a table or the floor. Spread the reclaimed pieces of fabric out, one at a time, on the foundation fabric with wrong sides together. Pin through both layers around the edges. Pin here and there inside the pieces if they are large, so that the top fabric lays flat. Cut completely around the fabric as though you were cutting out a pattern.

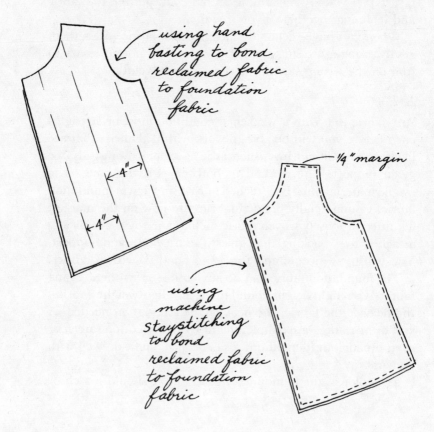

using hand basting to bond reclaimed fabric to foundation fabric

¼" margin

4"

4"

using machine staystitching to bond reclaimed fabric to foundation fabric

Using a single thread, hand baste the two pieces together at intervals—rows of basting about four or five inches apart, as shown in sketch. Or use the sewing machine and a normal-size stitch to staystitch around the enti e piece, ¼″ from edge; if piece is large it may be desirable to work a few rows of hand basting in the center. Whichever method you use, pause now and then to make sure the two layers of fabric are smoothly together.

Sometimes it is necessary to bond only the area of fabric on which you will work. For instance, suppose a band of contrasting fabric is to be inserted in a knitted shift (or other garment —this is a good way to lengthen skirts or tops or jackets). It is necessary to bond the knit both above and below where it will be cut, but nowhere else. Cut foundation fabric 4 to 6 inches wide and long as necessary to fit around the garment. Use tailor's chalk or pins to mark the cutting line on the right side of the knit. Place the foundation strip on the wrong side, center it on the marked cutting line, and pin in place at top and bottom. Run a row of hand or machine stitching ¼″ above and ¼″ below the marked cutting line. Now you are ready to cut through both knit and foundation strip; the knit will not ravel. This type of partial bonding is also useful in working with lace.

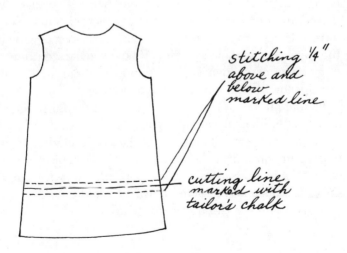

stitching ¼″ above and below marked line

cutting line marked with tailor's chalk

If an antique fabric has its own lining, and the lining is still in good condition, it may be used as the foundation. A brocade piano shawl, for example, may simply be basted to its own lining. The padding, if there is any, may be left in place between the brocade and the lining if a heavier garment is desired; or it may be removed. This is a matter of personal taste. I like to keep the padding whenever there is one; the resulting garment will have more "body," hang more stiffly from your body, and wear better.

After you have bonded your fabric to a foundation, you will work with both layers as though they were one. Cut and sew right through both layers, ignoring the basting or stay stitching. After your garment is completed, it is a simple matter to remove the basting stitches. Staystitching will be hidden in the seams, and not have to be removed.

After individual sections of your garment have been cut out — fronts, sleeves, and so on — it is a good idea to staystitch around them ¼″ from the edge.

*Piecing: Making More From Less*

You have decided on the new garment to be made, laid out your pattern on your fabric, and find that you are short. You need just a few inches more to finish a sleeve, make a waistband, or provide for a reasonable hem allowance. What should you do? Abandon the project? Never! Surely you will have a few scraps, irregular in shape, left over after you cut the garment segments out. Here is how you can combine them to give you extra inches where you need them, and here also are tips for finding extra yardage elsewhere.

First of all, lay out your pattern so that the fabric shortages occur in "hidden" areas only. On a skirt this would be the hem allowance and waistband. On a jacket it might be at the underarm seam, near the neckline if it will be hidden under a collar, the hem allowance, or perhaps the front overlap. On a sleeve it would be the hem allowance, or the bottom if there is to be a cuff, or the underarm seam.

26

First of all, try to eliminate some areas of your design. Certainly you will not waste precious fabric on facings. Instead plan on making a decorative lining; cut it in the same size and shape as the top fabric and bring it out to the very front edge of the coat or jacket (follow the directions for any of the reversible garments in Part III—Basic Styles #4, 5, 6, 7, or 11).

You might save fabric by redesigning a sleeve to make it shorter and/or narrower. Redesign a skirt to make it less full —a flaring A-line, for example, can become less exaggerated. Or a skirt can be redesigned to eliminate its waistband; after the skirt is put together, sew a length of grosgrain ribbon, $7/8''$ wide, to waist seam allowance of skirt; turn to inside and blind stitch in place. This will give you support where you need it, the skirt will sit smoothly on your hips, and you will save valuable fabric.

Grosgrain ribbon can also help you extend the length of a hem allowance. If your fabric gives you even as little as $3/4''$ in this area, you can add on ribbon to make the hem as deep as necessary for the skirt to hang well —2 to 3 inches is customary. Simply attach the ribbon as though you were attaching seam binding, and hem it as though it were your skirt fabric.

You can eliminate the front overlap of a coat or jacket by redesigning the closing so that the left and right fronts meet in the center, using frogs, zipper, or hooks and eyes as fastenings.

When you cannot redesign or add ribbon it is necessary to piece. Although this takes a little work and a great deal of patience, it is not frighteningly difficult. Lay out your scraps on a table in front of you, and try to fit them together to make larger pieces. Look closely at each piece to determine which way the threads of the fabric are running. When two pieces are sewn together the threads should run in the same direction. You will not be able to attach a bias edge to a straight edge. The bias piece is cut diagonally across the threads of the fabric, and has a lot of stretch and flexibility; it will not hold its size or shape. Trim the pieces to be matched, if necessary, so that straight edges will fit together. You may have to pull a few

27

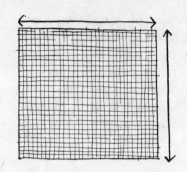

fabrics are made up
of threads crossing each
other at right angles

pieces cut on the
"straight of goods",
indicated by the
arrows, will hold
their shape.

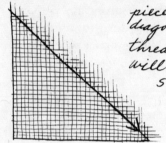

pieces cut on the bias
diagonally across the
threads of the fabric
will not hold their
shape

pull these threads out
to straighten edges of
fabric.

these two pieces can
then be joined to form
a larger piece

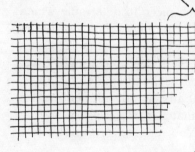
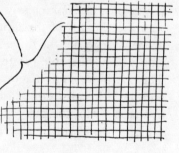

threads to straighten the edges. The pieces to be joined do not have to be exactly the same shape and size; only the two edges to be joined must be the same length.

When you have determined the best way to join your scraps, place the pieces to be sewn with their edges matching and their right sides together; seam ¼″ from edge. Press seam open on wrong side; press also on right side, moving iron up and down the seam and then at right angles across it. This type of pressing will make the seam as invisible as possible.

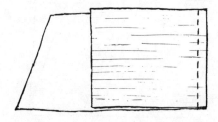

*place two pieces together with right sides facing, seam ¼″ from edge*

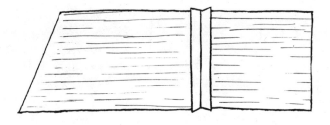

*view of wrong side of joined piece, with seam pressed open*

When joining several pieces together to form a larger piece, it is important for the seams to be lined up evenly. Suppose you have to join four scraps. Join the first two; then the second two. Press seams open as described above. Then, with right sides of the strips together, line up the seams evenly, placing a pin right through both seams to hold them in place. Sew the final seam across as shown in sketch; press open as described on previous page.

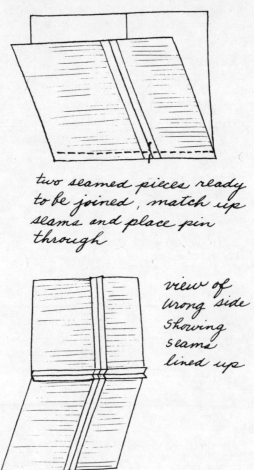

two seamed pieces ready
to be joined, match up
seams and place pin
through

view of
wrong side
showing
seams
lined up

In this way it is possible to piece almost anywhere it may be needed. The sketch shows one sleeve of a jacket being made from a brocade piano shawl. Notice how piecing was done so it would be hidden in the underarm area; notice also how additional piecing, necessary to lengthen the sleeve and provide a hem allowance, was done so that the horizontal seam line might form a mock cuff effect on the right side. In this particular case a ⅝"-wide piece of grosgrain ribbon was added at the bottom to extend the hem allowance, giving more body to the mock cuff. Even though the brocade had been bonded to its own lining, after piecing the entire sleeve was bonded by stay stitching to a second foundation lining, to give additional support and remove stress and strain from the piecing seams.

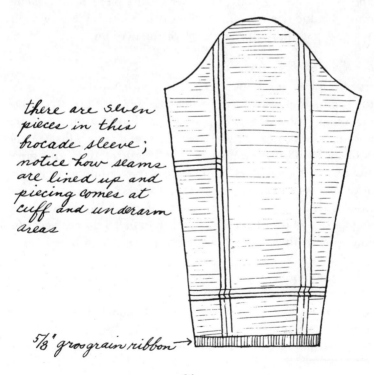

there are seven pieces in this brocade sleeve; notice how seams are lined up and piecing comes at cuff and underarm areas

⅝" grosgrain ribbon →

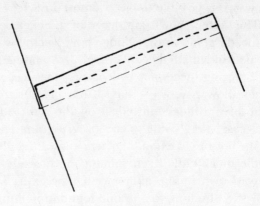

There is one piecing job where it is not necessary to make and press a seam, and that is when one piece of interfacing must be added on to another. Simply overlap the two by about ½″ and sew through the center of the overlap.

### For the More Experienced Sewer

Everything in this book except the next few paragraphs is for the beginner as well as the advanced sewer. But I really cannot recommend working with paisley and brocade shawls to the novice. The beginner should get some experience first, or she is likely to be discouraged by the length of time and great amount of patience such intricate work requires. It is not, however, necessary for one to be a professional dressmaker to work with these fabrics. I have seen women who knew sewing only fairly, who had perhaps fewer than half a dozen successful garments to their credit, tackle such projects with wonderful results.

For the more experienced sewer, then, I'd like to add a few more tips on working with these fabrics. Most important is the way you lay out your pattern on the shawl. Let's take the brocade variety first, because these are all basically the same. They are large squares of about 46 to 48 inches in each dimension. An elaborate design in velvet and metallic threads is embroidered in one corner and up the two adjacent sides. One such shawl will make a short A-line skirt *and* a sleeveless side-closing jacket; *or* an evening-length skirt. Two shawls produce an elegant evening suit with two skirts. The drawings show the approximate pattern layout for these projects.

Paisleys, on the other hand, are almost never the same, but they do have some things in common. They are larger than the brocades. Usually the predominating color is an earthy orange-red or orange-brown. There is a gray or black central area, often roughly oval in shape. And the paisley design is laid out symmetrically around it. The problem with paisleys is to figure out how to center the design on the garment you will make. For instance, the back of a coat should have as its center

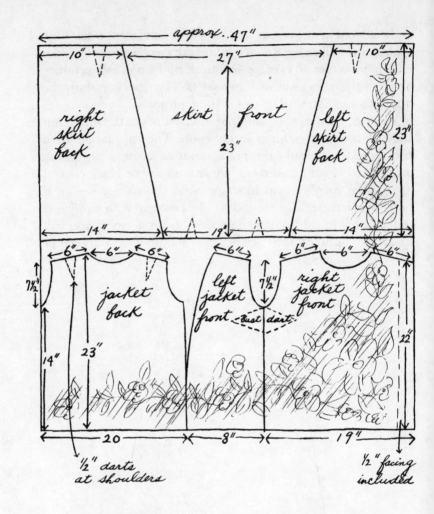

Cutting diagram for side-closing
sleeveless jacket and short A-line
skirt from a brocade piano shawl;
embroidered design comes mostly on
right jacket front.

the mid-line of the paisley design. It is a good idea to hold the fabric up against your body and center the design becomingly on yourself before laying out the pattern. Choose a pattern that has as few seams as possible. Try to match the paisley design along the seams. The black central area of the shawl is not used. Any leftover pieces can be used for hats, bags, shoes, and patchwork (see individual projects in Parts III and IV). Every paisley is unique, and anything you try to make from one of these will present its own individual problems, which only your skill and patience will be able to solve.

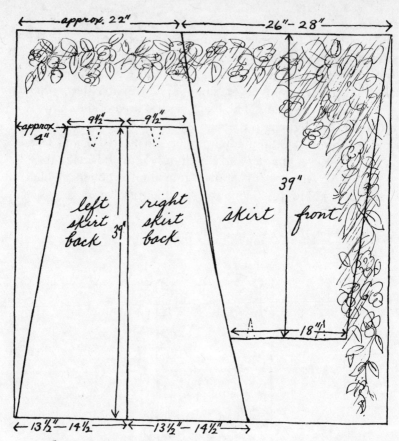

Cutting diagram for evening skirt
from second brocade piano shawl;
embroidery design rims mostly along
bottom and up right front.  Make a
matching bag from the leftover
fabric; or piece together to make
sleeves for the sleeveless jacket.
You have to play around with
your layout a bit to get the
maximum fullness in the skirt.

I believe in taking advantage of every possible shortcut and gadget in existence. I haunt five-and-ten-cent stores and notions counters, searching for things I can put to good use; and I've got a long list of indispensables. If you go on to make a number of the projects in this book, most of them will be indispensable to you, too. Here is my list, and some tips on the best way to use each item.

*silk-covered snaps:* These are larger than the ordinary snaps (and more expensive, too, but well worth it as a luxurious finishing touch) and are covered with silk in various colors. I use them to close coats, jackets, skirts, handbags, belts and almost anything else; I use them in place of zippers or hooks and eyes. They are decorative as well as functional, and make possible a very feminine gesture — flinging a coat or jacket or cape open in an instant. If you cannot find silk-covered snaps in the color of your choice, it is easy enough to dye the white or beige ones to any desired shade.

*silk-covered hooks and eyes:* These also make decorative closings for coats, jackets, waistbands. They are larger than the ordinary metal kind, and come in several colors. If necessary, dye to match.

*snappers and eyelets:* Kits containing no-sew snaps and eyelets in gold and various other colors, along with tools for attaching them, are available at most notions counters, and these can come in very handy indeed when you are making sportswear, children's clothes, and various accessories.

*buttons, buckles, and belts:* Shapes for making buttons from your own fabric come in several different sizes, with easy-to-follow directions for using them. There are also kits and instructions for making your own fabric-covered buckles and belts. It's easy to add custom details to clothes and accessories with these items.

37

*frogs:* These decorative closings come in many sizes, shapes, and colors, and provide an elaborate and frequently oriental effect.

*ready-made appliqués:* These are available in a multitude of designs — flowers and bugs, boats and planes, medallions, monograms, and even tiny triangular arrowheads to be used at the points of darts or to emphasize the inside edge of a buttonhole. They can all be glued or sewn in place. It is easy to dye white monograms to the color of your choice.

*drapery weights:* These are made of lead and are quite heavy, but because of the softness of lead they can be easily cut with a scissors. They come in several sizes, and may be either square or round. I like to use the ones that are about the size of a quarter, and I put them everywhere — in the hems of skirts as well as of coats and jackets, where they help a garment hang straight and keep its shape. They can also be used at the center of a wide neckline to make it drape gracefully. Sew weights as though they were buttons, over and over the center bar, to the inside of a hem, or to the neckline facing. If they are to be used on sheer or lightweight fabric, first cover the weight with a small piece of fabric to pad it, and then sew it, fabric and all, to the inside of the hem.

38

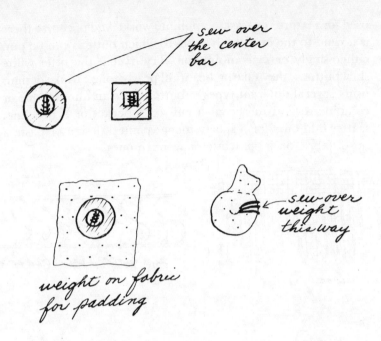

sew over
the center
bar

weight on fabric
for padding

sew over
weight
this way

*fringe, braid, and other trimmings:* I use these all the time, for contrast and for camouflage. A basic upholstery braid about ⅝″ wide comes in a wide variety of colors. Ball fringe also is widely available; if the color you need cannot be found, simply dye white or ecru. Cut the balls off and use them as flower appliqués or pompons. Decorative ribbons, in Roman stripes or Swiss embroidered, and ordinary satin, moire, grosgrain, and velvet ribbons come in a vast array of widths and colors. I use a great deal of lace, ⅝″ wide, in many colors, instead of seam binding. (Conventional seam binding is one notion I *never* use.) Other, more decorative laces come in varied widths, colors, and materials. There are cotton eyelet, ruffled, and embroidered varieties. Ready-made bias bindings also come in many colors and in wide as well as narrow widths; even gingham checks are available. Iron-on suede and corduroy and denim patches, in a selection of colors, can be cut out and

39

used for texture contrast in appliqué work. And of course there is no end to the imaginative uses to which buttons can be put, either singly or in combination. Try dyeing the little white shirt buttons: they take on beautiful pearly tones. Make designs using several different types of buttons: use an unusual one or combine several to accent a cuff or a pocket or a neckline; scatter odd ones for a sporty touch; paint a design or paste a bit of fabric on large white or wooden ones.

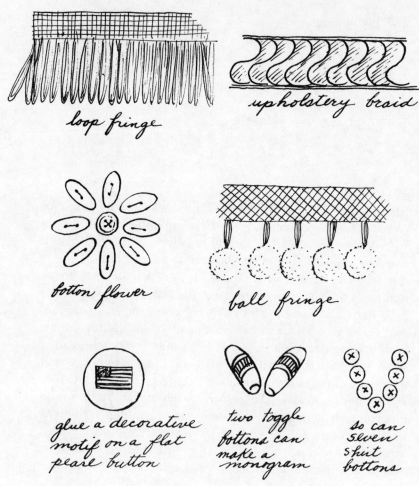

loop fringe

upholstery braid

button flower

ball fringe

glue a decorative motif on a flat pearl button

two toggle buttons can make a monogram

so can seven shirt buttons

*beads, bangles, bugles:* And paillettes, spangles, sequins. Just sew on these bits of glitter for a grand effect. Inexpensive necklaces are often a good source of unusual beads that can be used to accent necklines or bring sparkle to any part of a garment.

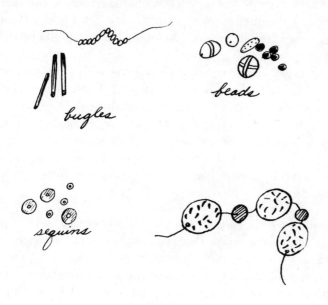

bugles

beads

sequins

*interfacing:* I use lots of interfacing to give shape and body to a loose-fitting skirt, coat, or dress. It comes in various widths, and in white, natural, and black.

*felt-tipped marking pens:* Now available in every color under the sun, and a few phosphorescent shades, too! Wonderfully handy for camouflage — I have a pink silk shirt that looks like ten times its value since I took a dark rose marker and drew leafy vines all over it to hide a stubborn stain. I use these markers for bringing out the faded color even in antique fabrics; or for "faking" a bit of old embroidery that might have been worn away. They can even match up zippers and snaps in an emergency.

41

*glue:* You need a strong, white glue-anything kind of glue — a little of it will go a long way in attaching one fabric to another. One of the best is *Sobo*, widely available at notions counters.

*spray paints:* These are as necessary to me as needle and thread, especially the gilt and clear varnish varieties. I gild all sorts of things — wicker baskets and hat boxes, walnut shells and empty thread spools. I weave narrow velvet ribbon through small plastic berry containers and then spray with gold paint — the result is a lovely dressing-table catch-all. It can be matched to a wastebasket of wider ribbon worked through large wicker or plastic baskets. To gild or spray with any color, or with clear varnish: place article (or articles — I do several at a time) to be sprayed on a layer of newspaper on the floor; use masking tape to put up a backdrop of more newspaper to protect your walls; and follow directions on the can.

*general sewing equipment:* I use pins by the boxful; keep several cloth tape measures handy so one is always within reach; have good sharp shears, pinking shears, and a couple of pairs of small sewing scissors. A seam ripper is indispensable. Everything else, including threads in several colors, can be acquired as you go along. In no time at all you will probably have quite an accumulation.

### Dyeing

I always have packages of dye in several colors on hand. It is not necessary to use the whole package to dye small items, like silk-covered snaps, zippers, and even gloves. I use an enameled saucepan or small basin, a spoonful or two of dye, and about a quart of hot water. Wear rubber or plastic gloves, and work the dye through with your fingers. Colors can be combined; you will have to experiment. For instance, a little brown added to gold may give you just the right shade of antique gold you are looking for; a little red might perk up an orange. Test the colors by dipping a scrap of fabric — any fabric, even a piece torn from an old bed sheet or rag — into the dye.

*How to Follow the Pattern Sketches in This Book*

We will not be working from patterns, but from what I call pattern sketches, in making the projects in this book. I don't believe in patterns: they are too rigid, and don't let you use your imagination. My pattern sketches are only suggestions: if you want to make something fuller, go ahead and add an inch or two; if you want to make something narrower or tighter, take away an inch. You can individualize everything you make or own.

Patterns aren't the only thing I don't believe in. I don't believe in basting, either, and I almost never do any. I pin everything — I use pins by the bushel! — before I sew. When I make something for myself I pin, pin, pin — and then I try it on, and then I pin some more, until I get just the fit and shape I want. Then I can do my sewing all at once, and never have to rip out basting threads. Since most of these garments are easy fitting, you won't have to strip down to your underwear to try them on. Just slip them over your clothes; keep trying on and pinning until you get the fit and shape *you* want.

I begin pinning even before I cut my fabric, and you will too when you follow my pattern sketches. Mark all measurements with pins; then cut as indicated. (If you prefer you can use tailor's chalk to mark your fabric for cutting.)

For instance, to follow the pattern sketches for Basic Style #1 in Part III, you should fold the fabric in quarters as shown

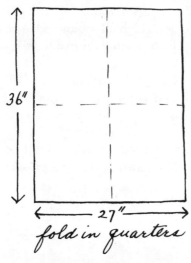

36"

←——— 27" ———→

*fold in quarters*

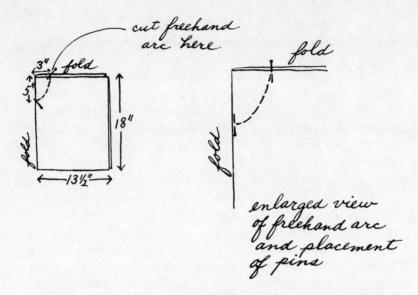

cut freehand
arc here

3" | fold

fold

18"

←——13½"——→

fold

enlarged view
of freehand arc
and placement
of pins

and place in it *two pins only*, one 3 inches from the folded corner along the shorter side of the folded fabric, and the other 5 inches from the corner along the longer side. Then cut freely in an arc between the two pins. (If you are afraid to cut free-hand, I hope you will learn not to be by trying it a few times; but if it really has you worried the first time use a pencil or tailor's chalk to first mark the curve on which you will cut.)

Now open up the folded fabric and try slipping it over your head through the opening you have just made. If the opening is too small to go easily over your head and hair-do, cut it just a little larger — ¼ or ½ inch all around. Don't bother marking this fraction of an inch: train your eye to tell you. Then try it on again.

It may take a while for you to get used to this free-and-easy way of cutting. If you are nervous at first, and afraid to ruin good fabric, try my method out on an about-to-be-discarded bed sheet. The results will surprise you, and give you confidence to cut into your good material. But if you are still hesi-tant, and feel more comfortable using a paper pattern, simply

44

follow the above directions to transfer my pattern sketches to tissue or wrapping paper. Use the resulting paper pattern to cut your fabric.

You can even cut a perfect circle of any size using this same freehand method. First determine the radius of your circle. If you want a circle 10 inches in diameter, the radius will be half that, or 5 inches. You will need a square of fabric, the length and width of which should be equal to or greater than the diameter of your circle. Next fold the fabric in quarters. With one hand hold a pencil at the beginning of a ruler or tape measure and hold a finger of your other hand the same number of inches as the radius away from the pencil. At this point place your ruler at the folded corner of the fabric and pivot the pencil end of the ruler around in an arc, marking the fabric in several places with the pencil or with pins as you pivot. This technique will work with something as big as the floor-length circle skirt (Transformation #5 in Part IV) or with something as small as the child's ruffled bonnet (Basic Style #15 in Part III).

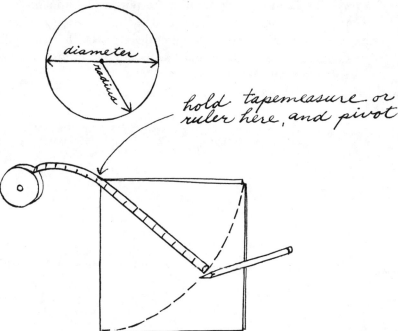

Using this basic method of pinning and cutting, you will be able to cut even much more complicated garments without using a paper pattern. The one thing that might give some trouble is a set-in sleeve. This feature occurs in only one of the styles in Part III, a variation of the tent (Basic Style #9). If you have trouble with sleeves, it is quite all right to use a commercial paper pattern as a guide.

### In the Rest of This Book

Finally, a word about the organization of the rest of this book. In Part III are directions for fifteen Basic Styles, most of which have at least one variation. Many have several. All are easy to make, but the first five are extra easy, and it might be a good idea for you to start by working on one of them, so you can get accustomed to my method. In Part IV you will find what I call Transformations — new things to make, original things to create from inexpensive and ordinary materials. Part V is full of ideas for gifts, accessories, and items that might be sold at a bazaar. Part VI is a How-To Glossary, with instructions for everything from making appliqué to putting in zippers.

After you have worked on several of these projects, I guarantee that you will know my basic ideas so well that you will be designing, too, using all my techniques and even adding a few of your own. And that is just what I want.

# Basic Styles and Variations

Here are fifteen of my favorite designs, and dozens of variations you can ring on the basic fifteen. Try them all, in different fabrics. Combine them for two- and three-piece costumes. And let my suggestions be only a starting point for your own ideas.

## Basic Style #1: POPOVER BLOUSE

This blouse (which can become a dress, house dress, and an at-home gown as well) is the easiest thing in the world to make. All you need is one small piece of fabric. You cut only at the neckline. Make it in whatever length you choose; it is the perfect top to wear with shorts or slacks. Make it extra short to wear with hip-huggers and a bare midriff. Make it fingertip length. Let it grow to just above your knee for a swinging little dress. And just about any fabric you choose will work: splashy cotton prints, bonded knits, acetate jerseys (for dress length); with matching or contrasting trim — slinky silk fringe or stiff yarn fringe, narrow flat braid or pompon braid.

The same fringe or braid can also be used at the very edge of the hem of the blouse or dress-length popovers, or a few inches above the hem of the dress or full-length popovers.

These longer versions can even carry several parallel rows of trim at and near the hem. Ball fringe is particularly effective on them.

The A-line popovers were designed not by me, but by a non-designer friend who got the idea for this variation after making several of the basic popovers. I like her idea so much that I'm including it here.

Blouse

Dress

Full Length

You will learn several basic things as you make this blouse:

1. How to measure and place a bust dart.
2. How to use trimmings to conceal and decorate at the same time—I call this camouflage, and I do it on practically everything I make.
3. How to use weights to make a garment hang properly.
4. And how one basic style can become several different garments.

## POPOVER BLOUSE

*materials*

¾ yard 36″ fabric
1 yard trimming (fringe or braid)
4 yards ½″ ribbon lace
8 weights (about the size of a quarter)

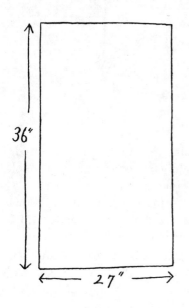

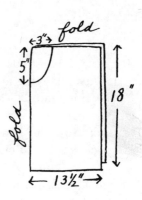

1. To cut head opening, fold fabric in quarters and cut as shown in sketch. See cutting directions in Part II. Try on; if head opening is too small, cut it ¼" to ½" larger all around.
2. Pin up hem to desired length.
3. Pin darts; try blouse on inside out. Pinch fabric together at the sides of bust. The dart will taper from next-to-nothing at the point of greatest fullness to about ¾" at the side edge. Sew, stitching from edge to point (when you sew a dart by machine, run your stitching right off the point of the fabric, sewing a few stitches beyond the point).

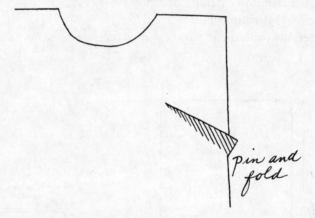

*pin and fold*

4. Leave blouse inside out and pin sides together 1½" from edge for seam, leaving approximately 8" free at top for armhole. Sew side seams. Seam allowance becomes armhole facing.
5. Place weights evenly around hem, four in front and four in back. Stitch to hem allowance only so that weight will be concealed inside of hem. Sew as shown.
6. Stitch ribbon lace to raw edges of seam allowance and hem. Sew lace down, making hem and finishing seams and armhole facing. Catch only one or two threads of outside of blouse as you sew.

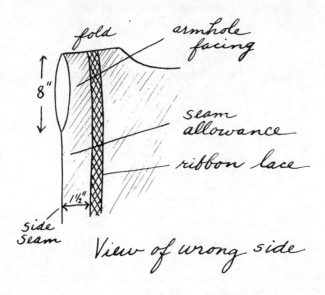

fold

armhole facing

8"

seam allowance

ribbon lace

1½"

side seam

View of wrong side

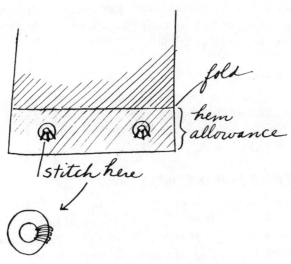

fold

hem allowance

stitch here

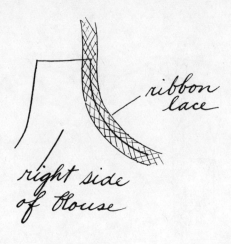

*ribbon lace*

*right side of blouse*

7. With right side of blouse facing you, stitch ribbon lace to neckline, overlapping about ¼". Turn lace to inside for neck facing and sew down.

8. Turn blouse right side out. Pin trimming around neckline and sew down. It will hide the stitches you made when sewing the neckline facing.

## POPOVER DRESS

You will need a piece of fabric 2¼ yards long and ¾ yard wide. Follow directions for popover blouse, above, and turn up hem to whatever length is desired — tunic, fingertip, mid-thigh, knee.

## POPOVER AT-HOME DRESS

For a full-length popover, use 3¼ yards of fabric, ¾ yard wide. Make a simple tie belt (instruction 11 for Drawstring Dress, Basic Style #10) from an extra piece of the same fabric, or from contrasting fabric.

## A-LINE POPOVER — Dress Length

Use 2½ yards of 36″ material, and fold and cut as shown in sketch. Follow directions for Popover Blouse, above.

## A-LINE POPOVER — Full Length

Use 3½ yards of 36″ fabric, and fold and cut as shown in sketch. Follow directions for Popover Blouse, above. For an Empire effect, tie a wide or narrow belt of the same or contrasting fabric high up on dress.

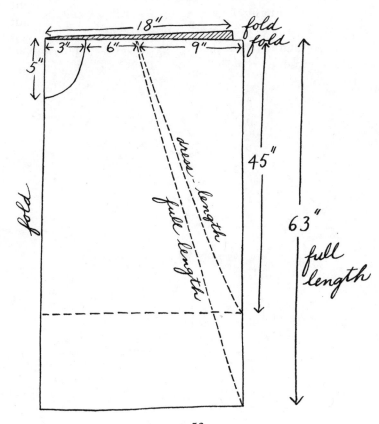

53

# Basic Style #2:
# DOLMAN-SLEEVED
# BLOUSE

Here is another one-piece-of-fabric blouse that can be made almost instantaneously and that grows in length to become almost any kind of dress you wish. It even becomes a little jacket. Once again, braid or fringe trimming can be used to highlight or play down the neckline.

The basic pattern is for an oval neckline, over-the-head blouse. The neckline can be changed to square and even V-shaped. And the basic blouse can open cardigan style in front to become a jacket with a button or snap closing, flaring out in back from an inverted pleat at the neckline. And you can make it reversible.

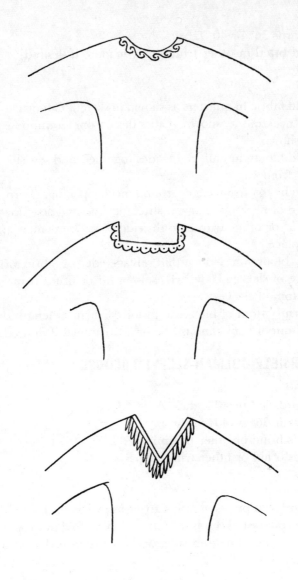

## DOLMAN-SLEEVED BLOUSE

*materials*

1½ yards 36″ or 40″ fabric
1 yard braid or other trimming (or more if desired)

*how-to*

1. Fold fabric in quarters as shown in sketch. Cut oval opening for neckline as shown. Cut sides in one continuous curve as shown.
2. Fold blouse in half, right sides together, and sew side seams ⅝″ from edge.
3. Stitch ⅛″ from edge around neck opening. Turn under edge of neck opening on stitching line and sew down. Pin braid or other trim at right side of neck opening and sew in place.
4. Try blouse on. Notice that selvage edge of fabric forms the edge of sleeve. If desired, sew braid or other trim around bottom of sleeves.
5. Turn bottom of blouse to inside for hem at length desired. Bottom of hem can also be braid trimmed if desired.

## REVERSIBLE DOLMAN-SLEEVED BLOUSE

*materials*

1½ yards 36″ or 40″ fabric A
1½ yards 36″ or 40″ fabric B
2 yards braid or other trimming A
2 yards braid or other trimming B

*how-to*

1. Place both pieces of fabric together, wrong sides facing. Pin if necessary to keep from slipping. Now fold in quarters and cut out neckline and sides as in instruction 1 for the basic style, above.

2. Separate fabrics, and follow instruction 2 above on fabric A unit. Stitch around neckline ½ inch from edge. Repeat for fabric B unit.

3. Place fabric A and fabric B units together, with wrong sides facing. Turn neckline edges in on stitching line, pin and sew both units together at neck edge. Pin braid or other trim around neck edge on both sides and sew in place. Pin braid to edges of sleeves and sew in place, stitching through both fabrics and both braids at the same time.

4. Try blouse on. Mark for hem length. Turn hem allowances to inside, between fabrics A and B. Stitch bottoms of hem together. Braid can also be applied to bottom of hem if desired.

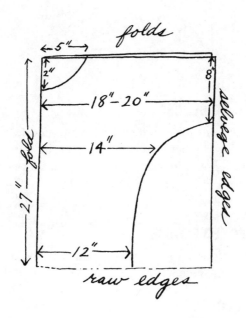

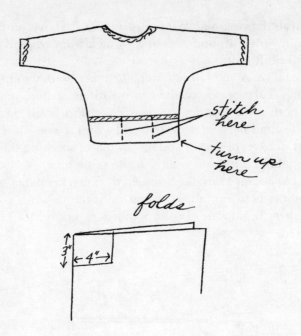

## POCKET-EDGED BLOUSE

Follow instructions for either of the two previous blouses. Instead of turning the hem inside, turn it to the outside to form pockets. Stitch down in four places to form six pockets, three in front and three in back, as shown in sketch. Top of pocket can be outlined with braid.

## SQUARE-NECKED BLOUSE

Follow instructions above, cutting square instead of oval neckline as shown in sketch.

## V-NECKED BLOUSE

Fold fabric in quarters to cut sides. Unfold; then fold in half lengthwise to cut neckline as shown. Follow instructions for blouses as above.

# DOLMAN-SLEEVED JACKET

*material*

1½ yards 36" or 40" fabric A

1½ yards 36" or 40" fabric B to make jacket reversible or
for lining

1½ yards interfacing

2 yards braid or other trimming

1 or more silk-covered snaps as desired

3 yards ½" ribbon lace (for lined jacket)

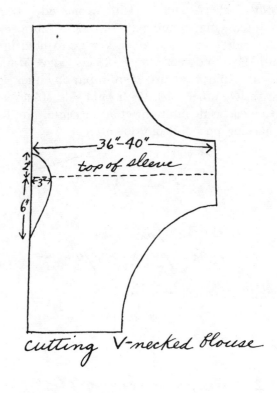

*cutting V-necked blouse*

59

1. Fold and cut top and lining fabrics as for Reversible Dolman-Sleeved Blouse, above. With both cut pieces together, unfold and then fold lengthwise in half. Cut for front opening along fold as shown in sketch.
2. Fold and cut interfacing the same way.
3. Place fabric A and interfacing together, with the wrong side of fabric A against the interfacing, and follow basic instruction 2. Repeat with fabric B.
4. Stitch ⅛″ from neck edge on fabric A and interfacing. Repeat for fabric B.
5. Place both jackets together, with wrong side of fabric B against interfacing, pinning the layers of fabric together along the side seams and at neck edge to hold in place. Fold in half to find center back of neck edge. Mark exact center with a pin. Measure 2″ from pin on either side and mark with two other pins. With right side of jacket facing you, bring each side pin to meet at the center pin. Remove these marking pins and pin down pleat.

center back and
2 side pins in place

2 side pins brought
to center to form pleat

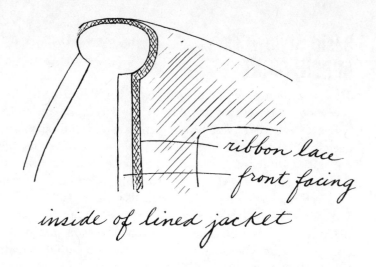

ribbon lace
front facing

inside of lined jacket

6. Pin trimming around sleeve edge and stitch down.

7. If jacket is to be reversible, turn neck edges to inside along stitching and pin together. Turn 1″ at each front edge to inside and pin, overlapping corner folds where neck edge meets front. Try on. Mark for hem. Turn hem allowance to inside and pin. Pin braid or other trimming around front and neck, starting at bottom of one front edge and going completely around neck, other front, and bottom of jacket. Sew trimming in place, stitching through all layers of fabric.

8. If jacket is to be lined, sew ribbon lace to right side of layered fabrics, going completely around front, neck opening, other front, and hem allowance. Turn neckline edge to wrong side and stitch down. Turn a 1″ facing to wrong side along each front edge and stitch down. Try on jacket. Mark for hem. Turn up hem allowance and stitch down. Pin trimming along front, neck opening, other front, and bottom. Sew in place.

9. Sew one fabric-covered snap in place near top of front opening. Jacket may be left open below neckline. Or sew additional snaps down front at 3″ intervals.

# Basic Style #3:
# APRON SKIRT

This is one of my very favorite designs. It is flattering to almost everybody, and is easy to make. The variations are endless. When Elizabeth Taylor brought me a wonderful old piece of needlepoint and asked me what I could make out of it, this is the skirt I designed for her. It was done in orange raw silk, with the needlepoint — a real museum piece worth several hundred dollars — set as an apron-like panel right in front. Fine upholstery braid edged the panel. Miss Taylor was delighted with it, as has been everyone else. It is just as lovely and interesting when made of a gay cotton print fabric with a straw place mat — yes, really, a place mat — for the panel. Long fringe outlines the place-mat panel on this skirt. I have also done this style in satin or taffeta with panels taken from pillow cases — either an old embroidered one or perhaps a fine lace one with lace outlining the panel.

This basic style makes a wonderful at-home skirt when extended to full length. Use a panel front for the full-length version, too. Or leave off the panel and appliqué, or embroider any motif you like. This skirt can be made for a special occasion. In fact, this basic style originated when, quite a few years ago, I decided to make a Christmas skirt. It was only a few weeks before the holiday, but I had just finished working on my regular line of holiday merchandise when I got the idea for it. I made up the basic style in green felt. In the very center I appliquéd a design of Santa Claus just going down a chimney, his bag overflowing with real, if miniature, packages. Small boxes were covered with gay fabric and tied with strips of narrow red ribbon. Some of the packages had burst open, and such gifts as a small string of seed pearls and sample bottles of French perfume, tiny dolls, a "diamond" ring from the dime store could be seen. I became fascinated with my Christmas skirt as I worked on it, and I kept adding a package here, and a miniature gift there, embroidering in between in a scroll pattern in different shades of green to enliven the texture of the felt skirt. I added a gay print lining in a firm but fine cotton fabric, and finally I decided that the skirt was finished. Arbitrarily, I decided to let Ehrlbacher's department store in Washington display it: Ehrlbacher's was a very good customer of mine. But it didn't get to the store until the morning of the very last day before Christmas. It was placed in a display window with a price tag of $375. And by the time the store had closed for Christmas Eve it was still there, unsold. I didn't know this, however, until several days later. Then I received a letter from a man who said he was a friend of the Ehrlbacher family, and had passed the store late on Christmas Eve, seen the skirt in the window, and telephoned the Ehrlbachers first thing Christmas morning. He had insisted that they open the store just for him so he could buy the skirt for his wife! I had a letter from his wife, too. She wrote me that she planned to wear the skirt every year at Christmas and to pack it away carefully for the other 364 days of the year, so that it might last long enough for her little girl to wear on Christmas, too.

I have made the identical skirt in blue denim with a red-and-white bandanna-print square kerchief for a panel; I call this version a Hobo Skirt (and it is very popular in my salon, too, at $175; I sell my customers a little blue knit shell to wear with it).

This skirt is basic in another sense, too. It illustrates several of my favorite techniques:

1. It contains an interfacing, for added body and wear. I find that garments made in a "sandwich," that is, with an interfacing layer between the top and lining fabrics, hang better, wear better, and last longer. They almost never need ironing.

2. It is fitted on you, to your figure.

3. The hem is turned up first.
4. All fitting and designing are done with straight pins — no tacking, no basting.
5. Lace is used instead of seam binding at hem and facing edges, and for hanger loops.
6. Silk-covered snaps (dye white ones to match if necessary) are used for easy-on, easy-off fastening.

Here, then, is the Apron Skirt, and a few of the variations you might like to try with it.

## APRON SKIRT

*materials*

3 yards 36″ top fabric

3 yards 36″ lining fabric

3 yards interfacing fabric

1 piece of contrasting fabric for apron panel, 12″ x 18″ or smaller, square or rectangular (pillow cover, place mat, needlepoint sampler, embroidered napkin, square cotton or silk kerchief — these are some possibilities)

2 yards of fringe or braid, or enough to go completely around the panel you have selected

10 silk-covered snaps in color to match or contrast with main fabric

4 yards of ½″ ribbon lace

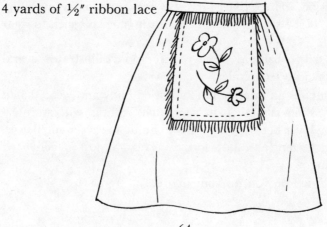

1. Cut or tear a strip 5″ wide and 36″ long from one end of each piece of fabric (top, interfacing, and lining). Reserve for waistband.

2. Place three large pieces of fabric together, with the interfacing between the wrong sides of the top and lining fabrics. Staystitch across long side ⅜″ from edge. Holding fabric top side up, attach ribbon lace at other long side.

3. Hold staystitched edge ½″ above your natural waistline, and mark off desired skirt length. Turn up hem, pin, and hem, sewing lace to lining fabric only.

4. Hold fabric top side up and attach ribbon lace at both short ends. Turn in 3″ evenly across each end for facing, and stitch lace to lining fabric only.

5. Fold skirt piece in half to get center top, and mark with pin.

6. Locate center of panel fabric you have chosen and pin in place ½″ below staystitching, matching centers of skirt piece and panel. Pin panel securely all around. Pin braid or fringe around panel. Stitch braid and panel to top skirt fabric.

7. Place skirt against yourself and pin tucks as shown in sketch, taking two or three close together on each side of panel.

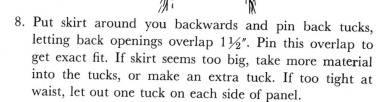

8. Put skirt around you backwards and pin back tucks, letting back openings overlap 1½″. Pin this overlap to get exact fit. If skirt seems too big, take more material into the tucks, or make an extra tuck. If too tight at waist, let out one tuck on each side of panel.

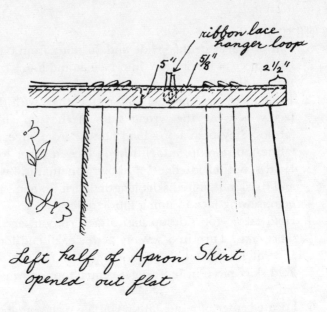

*5"*  *⅝"*  *2½"*

*ribbon lace hanger loop*

*Left half of Apron Skirt opened out flat*

9. Measure your waist. Place three waistband pieces together, interfacing between top and lining pieces, and pin in three or four places to hold together. Cut to your waist measurement plus 5". If your waist is 26", you will have a strip 5" x 31".

10. Place right side of waistband against right side of skirt, with 2½" hanging over at each end, and pin in place. To make hanger loops: cut two strips of ribbon lace 8" long and pin to inside of skirt at waistband on each side.

11. With wrong side of waistband facing you, stitch waistband to skirt ⅝" from edge. Turn waistband to inside of skirt, folding it in the center, and turn under ⅝" at free edge. Stitch down on inside of skirt.

12. Trim ends of waistband and turn inside. Stitch down.

13. Mark snap placement on one side of back facing with pins, having two pins in waistband about 1" from edge, and other pins evenly spaced at about 3" intervals, starting 1" below waistband and ending 1" from bottom of hem. Sew on snaps, matching them on other side of facing.

66

## HOBO SKIRT(S)

Make the basic apron skirt, using denim for the main fabric and a red or navy bandanna kerchief square for the apron panel. Or make it of red bandanna print fabric with a navy bandanna square panel. Edge with rickrack instead of fringe. Or, instead of or in addition to the apron panel, appliqué 3"-square "patches" of various cotton print fabrics on the skirt. Or cut the "patches" in the shape of flowers, watermelon wedges, butterflies, paper dolls — whatever occurs to you. If you like, draw pits on the watermelon, stems and leaves on the flowers, faces on the paper dolls with felt-tipped marking pens.

## SEWING SKIRT

To advertise your hobby, make the basic apron skirt in any fabric you like, but omit the apron panel. Instead, outline the shape of a panel with a cloth tape measure (these come in several colors) and sew down. Now fill in the panel area by sewing on buttons, miniature spools of thread (the kind that come in travel sewing kits), tiny pincushions, large snaps, large hooks and eyes — whatever you have on hand or can find at the notions counter. Make a small triangular pocket from a scrap of fabric; attach a bright ribbon to your sewing scissors, stitch other end of ribbon to skirt near pocket, and tuck scissors into the pocket. If you like to embroider, you can add small hoops and skeins of embroidery floss to your skirt.

## HOBBY SKIRT

Other hobbies can set the theme for a skirt design. The woman who is handy around the house might attach miniature tools, such as are sold in toy stores, to her skirt. A gardener might

68

appliqué flowers and draw in gardening tools with felt-tipped marking pens; she might add a large gardener's glove as a pocket. The Sunday painter could draw in a palette. The gourmet cook might use a novelty dish towel as a panel — one having recipes or decorative ovenware in its design.

## FULL-LENGTH APRON SKIRT

Use fabric that is 44″ to 54″ wide, and follow directions for basic apron skirt. Piece the interfacing if necessary. You will also need 5 yards of ribbon lace and 18 covered snaps. Make it in soft flannel or tweed, with a silk or taffeta lining. Omit the interfacing if the top fabric is firm, or if you prefer a softer skirt. Or make it in a linen or cotton for the summer.

## CHRISTMAS SKIRT

Make either the short or full-length versions of the basic apron skirt. Use red or green felt, omit interfacing and lining. Since felt is sold in widths of 60″ to 76″, you will need ¾ yard for the short skirt, 1¼ yards for the full-length one.

Follow instructions for basic apron skirt, but do not turn under facings or hem. Make waistband 3″ wide and sew directly to outside top of skirt. Let your imagination take over the decorating of this skirt. Perhaps you want to use a Christmas tree appliquéd on the front of your skirt, with buttons or dime-store "jewels" for lights, and packages at the base. Or an appliquéd Christmas stocking could have gifts tumbling out. You can buy Christmas stockings and Santa Clauses of felt in many notions and greeting-card shops. Cut candy canes out of white or pink felt and stripe them with red felt-tipped marking pens. Cut "boxes" out of felt and "tie" with sewed-on rickrack. Stitch tiny brass bells or large sequins onto a tree. Edge a chimney with rows of white mohair or angora yarn to represent snow. As you work on your Christmas skirt, one idea will lead to another. And you can always add a new holiday design every year.

# Basic Style #4:
# JIFFY SKIRT

Here is another quick and easy skirt, made from only one piece of fabric, and adaptable to several different styles and fabrics. I like to make it reversible (see instructions below) and then I get two skirts for the work of making one. This skirt combines with other basic styles to form several effective and quickly made outfits. The short Jiffy Skirt and the Jiffy Jacket (Basic Style #11) are a suit; wear the skirt and make the jacket three-quarter length for a smart costume. The Dolman-Sleeved Blouse (Basic Style #2) may be made of the same fabric as the Jiffy Skirt, or made of a contrasting fabric but given the same trim. A plain shell blouse may be trimmed at neck and armhole with the same braid as the skirt, or it may be completely covered with matching braid (as in the Fringe Blouse, Transformation #8).

Make the short Jiffy Skirt of a white basket-weave wool with white braid trim; line it in pastel multi-stripe silk. Or make it of gold terry cloth, unlined or with a cotton print lining, and trim it with bright orange yarn fringe. Make it in a textured black cotton with white trimming, reversible to textured white cotton with black. The full-length Jiffy Skirt could be of a muted plaid reversible to a solid color echoing one of the shades of the plaid.

## JIFFY SKIRT

Make it in an hour: only one piece of fabric to cut; only one seam to sew.

*materials*

¾ yard 44″ fabric
¾ yard ½″ elastic
2 yards upholstery braid in matching or contrasting color for trim

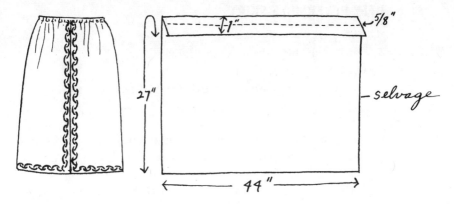

*how-to*

1. With wrong side of the fabric facing you, fold down 1 inch along long edge as shown in diagram. Stitch ⅝″ in from fold, forming casing for elastic waistband.
2. Place two short (selvage) edges of fabric together, right side in, and stitch ⅝″ from edge to form seam. Sew from bottom toward waistband, ending stitching when the waistband row of stitching is reached. Turn skirt right side out.
3. Use a safety pin to pull elastic through casing. Pin at one end. Try on skirt, pulling elastic to tighten waistband until skirt rests firmly but comfortably in place on top of your hip. Pin elastic at other end, leaving ⅝″ at each end and cutting off excess.
4. Turn skirt to wrong side. Stitch elastic in place. Sew casing edges together to continue seam.
5. Turn skirt right side out and try on again. Mark desired hem length. Take off skirt, turn wrong side out, and pin up hem evenly all around. Sew hem.
6. Turn skirt right side out. Sew on upholstery braid trim along seam and at bottom of hem as shown in sketch.

*Note:* This skirt will fit hip measurements up to 40″. For the narrow-hipped woman, use fabric 40″ wide, or cut or tear a 4″ strip from 44″ fabric. The large-hipped woman should use 46″ fabric.

## JIFFY REVERSIBLE SKIRT

*materials*

¾ yard each 44" fabric A and fabric B
¾ yard ½" elastic
4 yards upholstery braid, 2 yards each of two different colors

*how-to*

1. Place both pieces of fabric with right sides together. Stitch 1" from one long edge as shown in diagram. Open seam with fingers; press if desired.
2. Fold fabric right sides together so that the selvage edges meet; pin in several places. Put a pin through the stitching where the two ends of stitching meet. Sew seam ⅝" from edge. Press seam open.
3. Turn fabric so that fabric A section meets fabric B section exactly, wrong sides together, with first row of stitching exactly on top. Make another row of stitching ¾" from this top row to form casing, leaving two inches unstitched.
4. Insert elastic through opening in casing between layers of fabric; pin and try on as in step 3, above.
5. Overlap ends of elastic 1" and sew together, making several rows of stitching. Close up opening in casing.
6. Try on skirt; mark desired hem length on top layer of fabric. Take off skirt; pin hem allowance inside on that layer. Fold in and pin hem allowance on second layer to match. Hand or machine stitch two folded edges together.
7. Sew upholstery braid along seam and at bottom of hem on both layers of fabric, catching only the top layer with the needle, as in step 6 above.

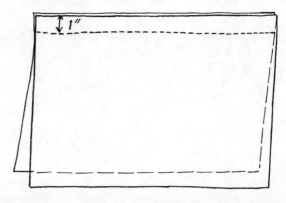

## JIFFY LINED SKIRT

Make this the same as the Jiffy Reversible Skirt, but fold both hem allowances under to lining side and hand sew to lining fabric only. Sew trim to top fabric only.

## JIFFY EVENING OR AT-HOME SKIRT

The basic Jiffy Skirt and the Jiffy Reversible and Jiffy Lined skirts can all be made full length for evening or at-home wear. You will need 1¼ yards of fabric and 3 yards of trim. The skirt can be made with a slit: leave the seam open for 7″ above the hem as shown in the sketch below. Press the seam allowance under at slit opening and catch it when sewing on the trim for a finished look.

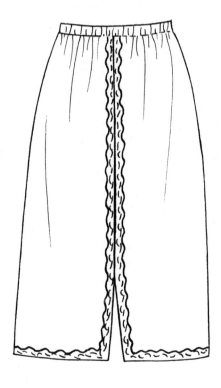

# Basic Style #5:
# COBBLER SHIFT

This "little nothing" dress hasn't got any side seams at all. It is made from one piece of fabric — you cut out the armholes and that's all there is to it. It has the easy-to-wear feeling of a cobbler apron, which gives it its name; but it can be as dressy as you like at the same time. And best of all, it can be made in only two hours from beginning to end. The trick is in the pinning.

I pin up the hem first — I like to see the shape of the dress as I work. And then I pin everything else — facings, shoulders, neckline — putting it on and taking it off and pinning and re-pinning if necessary until the shape is just right. Then when it is full of pins I start to sew.

This same basic style can become a Cobbler Apron if you like. Or a tunic, to wear with pants (for a quick hostess outfit, try it tunic length with the Party Pants in Part IV). It can lead a double life as a jumper. In black moire or crepe it is a perfect "little black dress." In brightly striped or flowered terry cloth it is equally perfect as a beach shift. A friend of mine had no other fabric on hand when a sewing mood struck her, so she made it from an old linen tablecloth. It is a perfect style for border or panel fabrics.

Trim it with heavy yarn fringe, with delicate sequins or beads, or with fine silk upholstery braid. Or leave it un-trimmed, and wear with a large glamorous pin, or an impor-tant necklace. Add a tie belt or a sash if you choose.

Leave it unlined, if you are in a real hurry, or line it with a contrasting fabric. But it is even better if you take the time to make it reversible.

And make it when you are too lazy even to open the sewing machine. It runs up almost as quickly by hand.

## COBBLER SHIFT

*materials*

1½ yards 44″ or 45″ fabric
5 yards ½″ ribbon lace
12 silk-covered snaps
weight (optional)
braid, fringe, or other trimming as desired

*how-to*

1. Take your hip measurement and add 8. Cut off fabric to this measurement. (If your hips measure 38″, add 8 and cut a 46″ length of fabric.)
2. Hold fabric up against you with selvage edges at top and bottom so that 2″ of fabric come above your collar bone. Mark approximate length of hem. Fold hem up to desired length and pin.
3. Turn in 2″ along raw edge for center back facing and pin.

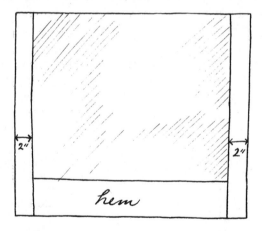

4. Fold in half and mark front center at top and bottom with pins.

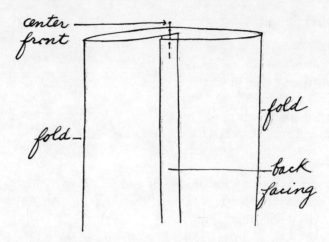

5. Fold so that back facings overlap each other and are centered over front center pins. Pin in place. Pin also at top of sides as shown. Check width of garment now. It should be half your hip measurement plus 2″. (If your hips measure 38″, width of folded shift should be 21″.)

6. Now fold again so that side tops are matched where you have pinned them. The front will be inside, the back outside.

7. Cut armhole openings as follows: Measure your shoulder breadth, add 1″ and divide by 2. (If your shoulder breadth is 13″, add 1, divide by 2=7″.) Leave this amount at garment top, and cut as shown in diagram.

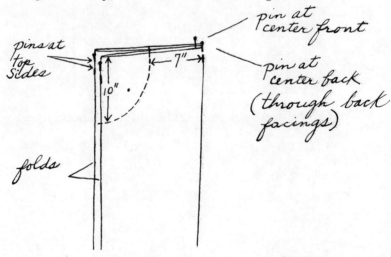

8. Turn neck and shoulder edges to wrong side, folding 2″ from edge to form facing. Measure 4″ from armhole at shoulder edges and pin. Overlap shoulders toward front or back, tapering from this point out to about 1″ at armhole edge, as shown. Try on.

9. Adjust shoulder line if necessary; remember that about ½″ at armhole edge will be folded under for armhole facing. Adjust neckline as desired. It naturally forms a bateau neckline as it is. It can be cut to scoop in front and/or back. For a draped effect, attach one drapery weight at center bottom of front neckline facing.

10. Sew ribbon lace ¼″ from armhole edges. Turn under and stitch down to form finished armhole. Sew shoulders down invisibly. Try on; check hem length and adjust if necessary. Sew hem. Sew back facings invisibly. Sew top halves of fabric-covered snaps at 3″ intervals on left back facing, placing them ½″ from edge and starting ½″ from top. Sew other snap halves on right back to correspond. Trim neckline, skirt bottom, and/or armholes if desired.

neckline

4″

center front

neckline facing

weight attached to neckline facing

## COBBLER TUNIC OR APRON

Make it exactly the same as the dress-length basic version, but, instead of turning the hem to the wrong side, turn it to the right side and stitch at intervals to form pockets all around as shown. Trim as desired.

## REVERSIBLE COBBLER

*materials*

1½ yards each of two fabrics, 44″ or 45″ wide
12 fabric-covered snaps
drapery weight (optional)
braid, fringe, or other trimming as desired

*cobbler apron*

1. Take your hip measurement and add 8. Cut off both fabrics to this measurement. (If your hips measure 38″, add 8, and cut fabrics in 46″ lengths.)
2. Place both fabrics right sides together. Fold in half so that raw edges meet; mark at top and bottom of fold with pins for center front.

3. Unfold. Fold twice so that raw edges overlap each other on top of center pins. Each raw edge should extend 3″ past marking pin. Use more pins to hold in place. Pin also at top of sides as shown. Check width of garment now. It should measure half your hip measurement plus 2. (If your hips measure 38″, width of folded shift should be 21″.)
4. Now fold again so that side tops are matched where you have pinned them. The front will be inside, the back outside.

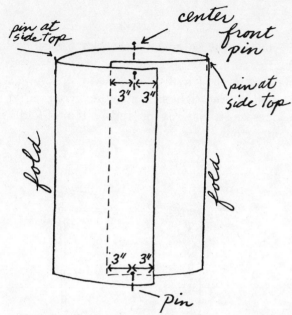

5. Cut armhole openings as follows: Measure your shoulder breadth, add 1″ and divide by 2. (If your shoulder breadth is 13″, add 1, divide by 2 = 7″.) Leave this amount at garment top, and cut as shown in sketch on bottom of page 68, cutting through all eight layers of fabric. Place pins at intervals along cut edges to hold.

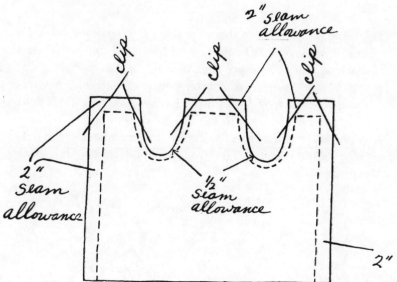

6. Stitch up back, across back neck, around armhole, around front neck, around other armhole, around other side of back neck, and down back, keeping lines of stitches the distance from the edges shown in sketch. Clip corners as shown in sketch.
7. Turn right sides out, rolling fabric along stitching until it lies flat. Measure 3½" from armhole edges and mark with pins. Overlap shoulders from these points as shown in sketch. Try on, pinning shoulders together. Pin to mark hem length.
8. Turn hem allowance to inside, and slip stitch invisibly at bottom. Slip stitch shoulders along overlapped areas. Sew fabric-covered snaps at 3" intervals down back, placing them ½" from edge and starting ½" from top, being careful not to stitch through both layers of fabric. Trim neckline, hem bottom, and/or armholes as desired.

*Note:* Snaps tend to pop open in the hip area on a slim skirt such as this one. To avoid this, overlap the right and left backs at center back and sew in place, seaming only from hem to just below waist.

To turn reversible garment hem neatly:

Spread seam open with fingers and fold hem allowance in so that seams of hem allowance and outside of garment lie flat on top of one another

# Basic Style #6:
# SANDWICH-SIGN DRESS

I call it that because that's what it looks like. It is another easy reversible dress. The second side has a border of the first side's fabric all around it. Making the dress reversible not only gives you extra chances to wear it, but gives the dress extra body so that it drapes gracefully. In fact, I like to add a third layer, of interfacing, so that the dress really stands out on its own.

I made my first Sandwich-Sign Dress from a teal-blue fabric printed here and there with white daisies, reversing to a pink

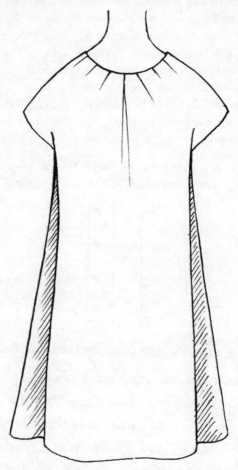

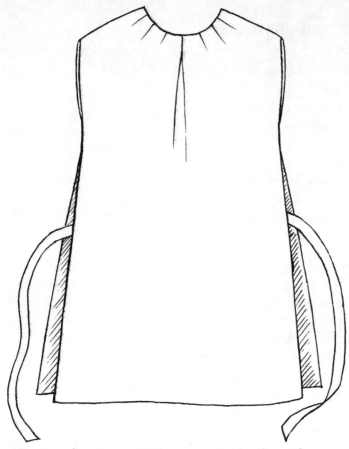

polka dot. I cut out all the extra daisies from the scraps of fabric I had left over, and appliquéd them along the neckline on *both* sides of the dress. And, browsing through some of the ready-made embroidered appliqués available at my favorite notions counter I found one in the shape of a bee. Just the thing to add to my daisies, I thought. And I did — a bright little bumblebee has just landed on a daisy near my left collarbone.

Make this in cotton fabrics of all kinds — denim, calico, hopsacking, ticking, flowery prints. Make it in knits or jerseys, brocades and wide-wale corduroys. But be sure to use the interfacing layer to give it body.

## SANDWICH-SIGN DRESS

*materials*
  2½ yards 44" to 46" *each* fabric A and B or 3 yards 39" *each*
    fabric A and B
equal amount of interfacing
6 to 8 weights

*how-to*
  1. Cut or tear fabrics so that you have one piece each fabric
     A and B 36" x 44"; one piece each fabric A and B 39" x
     44"; and two long strips of *either* A or B 2½" to 3" x 36".
  2. Cut one piece of interfacing 32" x 39" and one piece 29"
     x 39".
  3. Take larger pieces of fabrics A and B, and interfacing.
     Place together with interfacing centered between sides
     and even with other fabrics at top, as shown. Hold in
     place with a few pins. Fold all three layers in half length-
     wise.
  4. Cut front neckline and shoulders as shown.

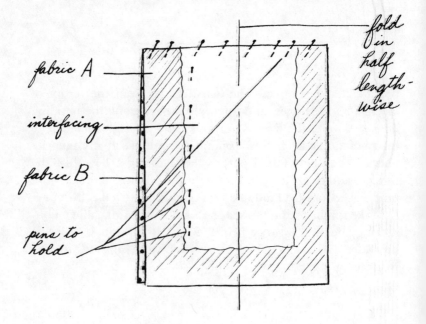

fabric A

interfacing

fabric B

pins to
hold

fold
in
half
length-
wise

cutting front
neckline and shoulder

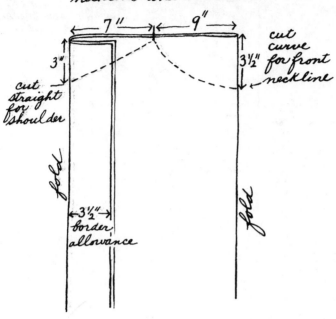

7″   9″

3″

3½″

cut
curve
for front
neckline

cut
straight
for
shoulder

fold

fold

3½″
border
allowance

Front

3½″   7″   18″

39″

Front
unfolded, it will look
like this

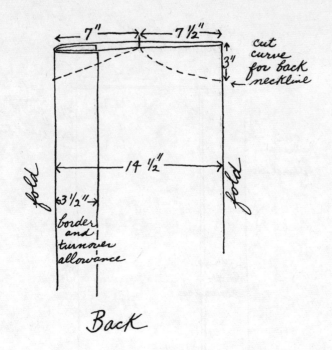

7"     7½"

cut
curve
for back
neckline

3"

14½"

fold          fold

3½"
border
and
turnover
allowance

Back

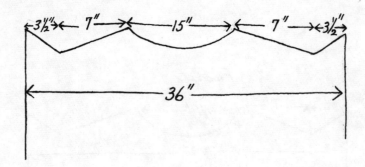

3½"  7"     15"     7"   3½"

36"

Back
unfolded, it will look
like this

86

5. Repeat step 3, using smaller pieces of each fabric and interfacing.

6. Cut back neckline and shoulders as shown.

7. Make fabric B unit: Place front and back of fabric B together so shoulders match, with right sides facing. Sew shoulder seams 1″ from edge; clip from edge to seam where border begins.

8. Make fabric A unit: Place interfacing back against wrong side of fabric A back; pin or baste across top to hold. Place interfacing front against wrong side of fabric A front; pin or baste across top to hold. Place unit A front and unit A back together with *right sides facing* (interfacing will be *outside*), and sew shoulder seams 1″ from edge. Clip from edge to seam where border begins. Remove pins or basting.

9. Place fabric B unit and fabric A unit together with right sides facing. Sew completely around neck opening ½″ from edge. Turn right sides out by pushing fabric B unit *through neck opening.* Use fingers to work fabric smooth along neck and shoulder seams.

10. Pin center pleat and side tucks at front and back neckline as shown. Note that an inverted pleat on the fabric B side becomes a regular pleat on the fabric A side. Likewise, a tuck that faces outward on the fabric A side will face toward the center on the fabric B side. Try on with fabric

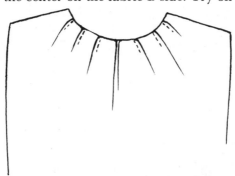

*front - fabric A-side*
*shows inverted*
*pleat and tucks face sides.*

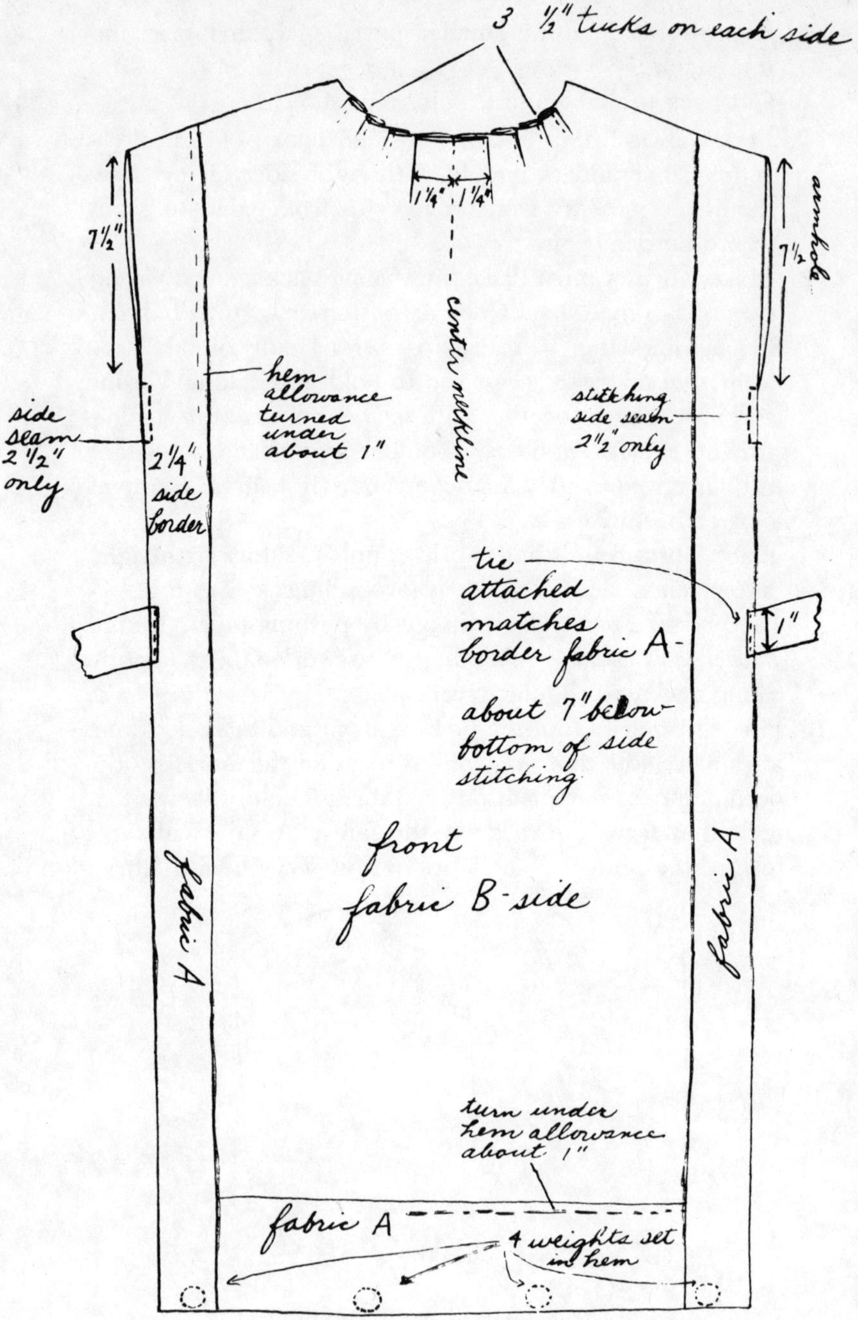

3 ½" tucks on each side

1¼"  1¼"

7½"

armhole

7½"

center neckline

side
seam
2½"
only

hem
allowance
turned
under
about 1"

2¼"
side
border

stitching
side seam
2½" only

tie
attached
matches
border fabric A

about 7" below
bottom of side
stitching

1"

front
fabric B-side

fabric A

fabric A

turn under
hem allowance
about 1"

fabric A

4 weights set
in hem

A side facing out to check whether neckline falls flat where you want it to. Take neckline in more by making larger pleats and/or tucks, or by adding more tucks. Make neckline wider by making smaller pleats and/or tucks, or by eliminating some tucks.

11. While trying dress on, mark desired hem length. It may be anywhere from 4″ to 8″ above the cut bottom of the dress. Pin across both front and back on hem line. Trim front and back hem allowances so that they are even at about 5″ to 6″ below hemline. Trim interfacing so that it ends just at desired hemline. Fold all layers to fabric B side on pinned hemline; use pins to hold. Sew weights to interfacing just above hemline, using 3 or 4 evenly spaced across each front and back. Turn under about 1″ at top of hem allowance; hem.

12. Sew pleats and tucks down, stitching vertically for about 1″ below neckline.

13. Fold side borders to fabric B side; turn under 1″ and stitch down.

14. Sew sides together for 2½″ to form armhole as shown.

*Back*

*fabric A side has pleats and tucks facing out towards sides*

*all tucks and pleats are stitched down about 1."*

## Back

fabric B side - has inverted
pleat 3/4" each side of center
and 2 center facing tucks on
each side.

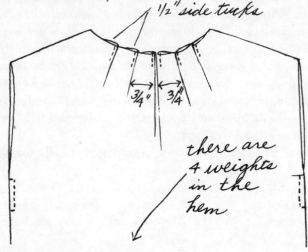

1/2" side tucks

3/4" 3/4"

there are
4 weights
in the
hem

15. Make ties: Fold each 2½" to 3" x 36" strip in half lengthwise and stitch all around ¼" from edge, leaving a 3"
opening. Turn; sew up opening. Attach ties to front sides
as shown, positioning them for high or natural waist as
you prefer.

*Note:* To make instructions clearer, I have been referring to a
"front" and a "back" to this dress, but it really doesn't have
them. Either side may be worn forward or aft. Try it both
ways!

leave opening

36"     2½"

fold     to make ties, stitch around
¼" from edge and sides.

# Basic Style #7:
# WISHBONE COAT

The shape of this little coat, with its deeply cut-out armholes, reminds me of a wishbone, hence the name. It is a versatile sleeveless garment, becoming a suit topper or an evening coat with equal ease. Because the sides are mostly open, it can be worn gracefully over the fullest of skirts. I make it reversible —using an easy sewing-machine method. It is very easy to make, too—each of the three pieces is finished first, and then they are put together with a bare minimum of hand sewing.

As for fabric, you are limited only by your imagination. Corduroy, cut velvet, tweed, denim, brocade, bonded jersey or knit—the fabrics you choose will tell you when to wear your coat. Get extra wear out of it by spraying it with a water repellent; a brocade theater coat that is rainproof is a wonderfully useful addition to any closet.

Make it full length to go easily over an evening dress. Or turn it into a tweedy jumper to wear with a turtle-necked ribbed wool sweater.

Use interfacing to give extra body to most fabrics, even though you are making it reversible. And set weights into the hem so it will always hang properly on you.

You can vary the details as you like—make it collarless, or with a little mandarin collar. Add pockets in varied shapes.

(You will have large scraps of fabric to use for these.) Buttons can glisten down the front of one side, with braid on the other, to hide the snap closing hidden in between.

## WISHBONE COAT

*materials*

2¼ yards each of two 36″ fabrics and interfacing
14 weights
12 silk-covered snaps (and/or buttons)
braid (optional)

*how-to*

1. Cut as shown in sketches. Note that neckline is cut 3″ deep in front, only 1½″ deep in back. Note that armhole cutout is deepest at about the middle (looking at it cut properly reminds me of a lady wearing a bustle).
2. Put back together first: Make a "sandwich" of your fabrics with the interfacing on top and the two fabrics with right sides facing each other beneath. Seam ⅝″ from edge all around, leaving only bottom open. Clip corners as shown; turn right sides out. (Interfacing will now be the "filling" in the "sandwich.")

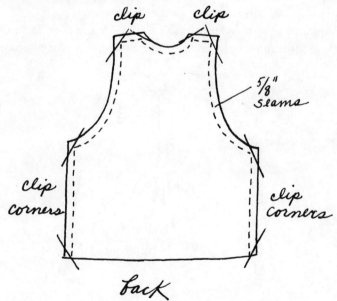

cut at
fold

front

← 3″ →

3″

18″

40″

7″

5″

10″

← 22″ →

back

fold

1½″

3″

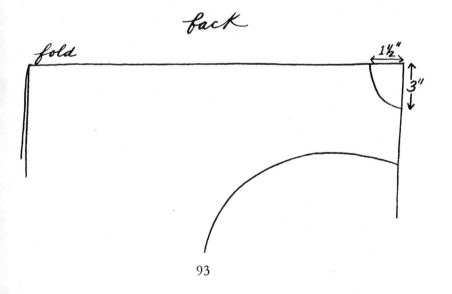

93

3. Repeat for both fronts.
4. Sew shoulder seams: *Either* stitch invisibly by hand, *or* overlap ¼″ and topstitch.
5. Try on. Determine hem length. Pin. Turn hem allowance to inside. Sew weights to hem allowance — 6 evenly spaced across back, 4 evenly spaced across *each* front. Sew bottom closed with invisible stitches (a tiny whip stitch is best).
6. Attach sides of coat at bottom of armhole opening: Tack together and cover tacking with a button or a bow. Or join with several 1″ lengths of sewing thread and work a buttonhole stitch over these threads, as shown.
7. Sew snaps at 3″ intervals down front. Cover with buttons if desired, on one or both sides. Or work machine buttonholes down one front edge of coat, and sew buttons on both sides of other front edge.

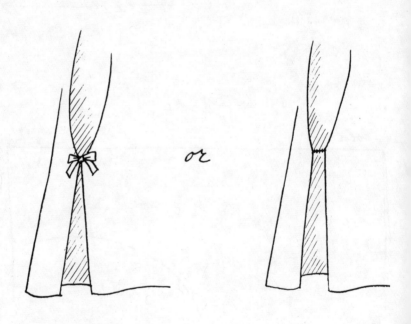

## EVENING WISHBONE COAT

*materials*

3¼ yards each of two 36" fabrics and interfacing
14 weights
12 to 16 silk-covered snaps (and/or buttons)
braid (optional)

*how-to*

Follow cutting directions for Basic Wishbone Coat, but making length of cut evening version 58" from shoulder to bottom. Sew snaps (and/or buttons) as far down front as desired; it is attractive to let the front remain open for 12" to 14" from hem. Sides may be attached in several places with a frog or braid closing or other decorative trim, leaving long slits at bottom.

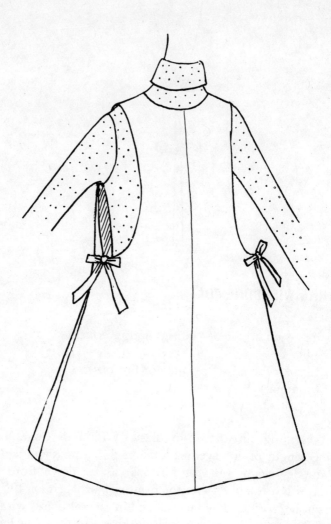

## WISHBONE JUMPER

Follow directions for Basic Wishbone Coat, but close up sides
completely, topping side seams with a bow.

# Basic Style #8:
# JUMPER COAT

Here's another sleeveless coat, with the popular tent silhouette. What you do with it is up to you. You can make it as full as a real tent, or narrower if you think it more becoming. It's a dress; it's a jumper; it's a costume-making coat over a dress or a skirt and sweater. In a short fingertip length it's a tent-tunic to wear with pants. In terry it's a beach coat. In chiffon or lace it's a cage, to make a gala style out of the simplest dress. A sleeveless tent-tunic of black chiffon over a skinny long-sleeved black crepe dress would be wonderfully smart and sophisticated for evening. And, of course, it's reversible (except in sheer fabrics, of course; if you choose these, get one that has some body to it — a bonded lace knit, or a starchy chiffon).

In making it you will learn yet another easy way to make a garment reversible. If you choose to do it without a lining or reversing fabric, you will apply a decorative lace seam finish. And you will learn one of my favorite tricks — using fabric-covered snaps as a decorative as well as functional touch on a reversible garment.

# REVERSIBLE JUMPER COAT

*materials*

3½ yards each of two 45″ fabrics and interfacing
12 silk-covered snaps

*how-to*

1. Cut back and two fronts from each fabric and interfacing, following cutting diagrams below. Cut backs first: place on front fabric leaving 2″ in front (to allow for center front overlap in finished garment) and use backs as pattern for cutting fronts. If a very full garment is desired, follow dimensions in diagrams 1A; for a less full version, follow diagrams 1B.

2. Match up and sew side and shoulder seams of top fabric. Repeat with reversible fabric. Repeat for interfacing.

3. If pockets are desired, cut them out of leftover fabric. For patch pockets, place on fronts of same fabric and sew in place.

4. Match up and sew side and shoulder seams of top fabric. Repeat for reversible fabric. Repeat for interfacing. You now have three separate "coats."

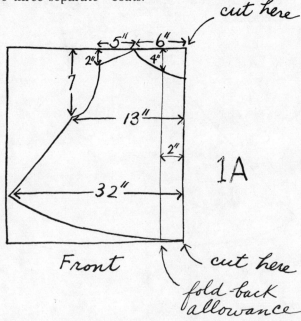

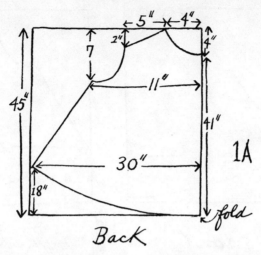

**Back**

5. Place these three coats together, right sides of both fabrics out and interfacing in between the wrong sides of both fabrics. Pin together through the seams to hold in place. Turn in ¼″ all around at neckline and armholes; pin as you turn. Stitch invisibly with a tiny whip stitch around neckline and armholes.

6. Try on; pin to mark for hem length. Turn under desired hem allowance; pin and stitch invisibly.

7. Turn both front edges in 1″; pin and stitch invisibly. Sew snaps at 3″ intervals down front. To use snaps decoratively on both sides of reversible coat, sew them together through both layers of each front as shown on diagram. (I like to use snaps in all different colors for this; the snaps that show add to the design of the garment.)

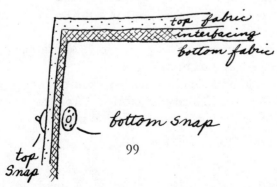

99

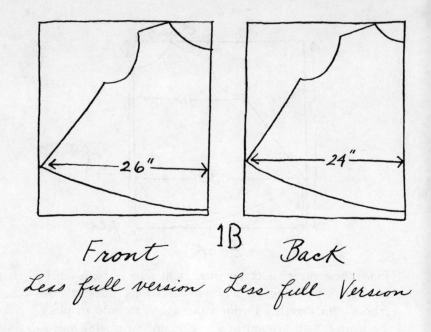

Front     1B     Back

Less full version    Less full Version

## SHEER FABRIC JUMPER COAT

*materials*

3½ yards of 45″ sheer fabric (chiffon, lace, etc.)
10 yards ½″ ribbon lace to match
12 silk-covered snaps to match

*how-to*

1. Cut out back and two fronts, following sketches 1A or 1B above.
2. Cut pockets, if desired, out of leftover fabric and sew in place.
3. Attach ribbon lace to each piece, overlapping it ⅛″ on fabric edges, except at bottom.
4. Sew side and shoulder seams; seam allowance should be ⅝″ from original edge of fabric, 1″ from edge of lace binding. Sew edges of seam binding to fabric.

5. Turn armhole edges in and hem down; catching lace only lightly in fabric.
6. Sew ribbon lace to bottom of hem allowance. Try on; pin to mark hem length. Turn up hem allowance and hem.
7. Pin neckline edge in ¼"; pin front edges in 1". Stitch down lightly, catching lace only in fabric.
8. Sew on snaps at 3" intervals.

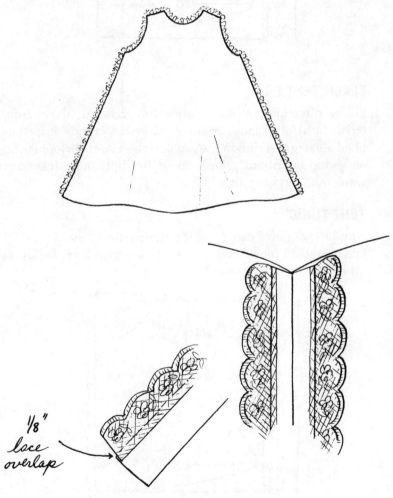

⅛"
lace
overlap

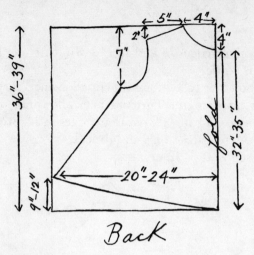

*Back*

## BEACH TENT COAT

Follow directions for Sheer Fabric Jumper Coat, above, using terry-cloth fabric and brightly colored — perhaps striped or plaid — grosgrain ribbon instead of ribbon lace. (Before sewing on grosgrain ribbon, preshrink it by dipping in lukewarm water and pressing lightly.)

## TENT TUNIC

Any of the above can be made tunic length; use 36″ or 39″ fabric, and 10 snaps. Follow cutting diagrams here. Follow all other directions as above.

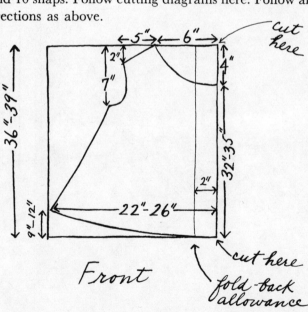

*Front*

# Basic Style #9:
# THE TENT

It's a coat; it's a dress; it's a coat-dress; it's a nightgown, a negligee, an evening gown, an at-home gown, a work dress, a house dress — it's a Tent! It's the smartest, easiest-to-wear silhouette that fashion has discovered, and now you can make it yourself from my favorite pattern.

This one is really flexible. I have one in an orange-y Banlon print, with a softly cowled neck and long sleeves, that I just slip into and live in. One of my favorite coats is a pink mohair tent, with a striped silk lining, and a large collar falling flat over the shoulder edges with a fine ribbon trim. I have a paisley tent, made from a wonderful old shawl, with a skirt to match. I have several sleeveless tents in fine cottons, linens, and silks; and my calico patchwork long-sleeved tent has softly striped velvet ribbon edging its collarless neckline and zippered front closing. This style is adaptable to any fabric and almost any trimming treatment. It is elegant in white satin, casual in a brightly striped heavy cotton, extraordinary in an upholstery brocade, practical in a soft knit or tweed. . . . The possibilities are, literally, endless.

However you decide to style your tent, it will need lots of fabric for a full, swirling, feminine effect. That is the beauty of it — it fits smoothly and easily on the shoulders, but falls in a rush of fabric to the hem. Let's make it sleeveless first, in an over-the-head style that won't ever muss hair; then add sleeves, pockets, and a front snap or zipper closing.

## SLEEVELESS COWL-NECK TENT

*materials*

3 yards 45″ fabric
3 yards ribbon lace

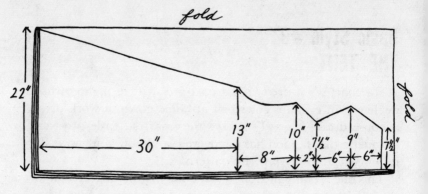

*how-to*

1. Fold fabric in half crosswise and in half lengthwise. Cutting *through all four layers of fabric*, follow cutting diagram.
2. Place two front pieces together with right sides facing and sew center seam. Repeat with both back pieces. Place front and back together with right sides facing and sew shoulder and collar seams.
3. Leave wrong side out and slip over head. Pin dart: Mark top of dart with a pin, just below and outside of the fullest part of bust. Start from side-seam allowance about 2″

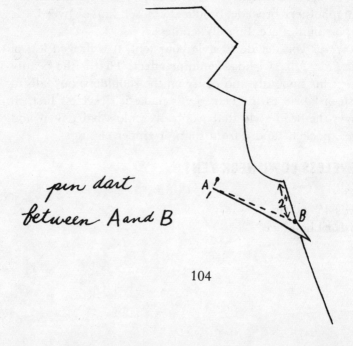

*pin dart between A and B*

104

below armhole and pin in fabric as needed, tapering to nothing at pin marker. (If you are small busted, you may not need a dart in some fabrics; try tent on and see how it falls *on you.*) Pin other dart to match.

4. Sew darts.
5. Even up back to correspond to new outline of front because of darts. With front and back together, pin along side-seam allowance at 5″ intervals, starting from hem. Pin also at underarm above dart. Trim off excess fabric in dart area so that front and back match. *Or:* Trim 1″ off across bottom of back. Pin front and back together at intervals within seam allowance and trim slight excess off front seam edges as necessary.

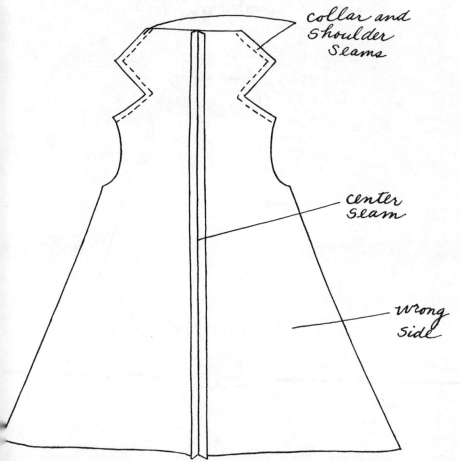

collar and shoulder seams

center seam

wrong side

6. Sew side seams.

7. Try on. Pin up hem to desired length. Sew ribbon lace at edge of hem allowance. Sew hem.

8. Sew ribbon lace at top edge of collar. Fold collar at fullest point so it has a double thickness. Sew lace-trimmed edge invisibly to inside base of collar.

9. Try on. Shoulders should just overhang the edge of your shoulder. Trim armhole, if necessary, to get this fit. Sew ribbon lace around armhole as a facing. Turn in ½″, and hem invisibly in place.

10. Trim, if desired, with braid, fringe, or ribbon around armhole, on collar, at hem, or wherever desired. For a mock fly front, sew a wide band of ribbon over the center front seam and sew buttons at intervals. The sketches show some of the possibilities.

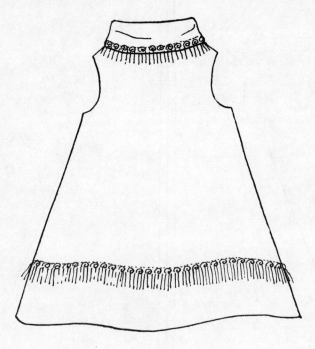

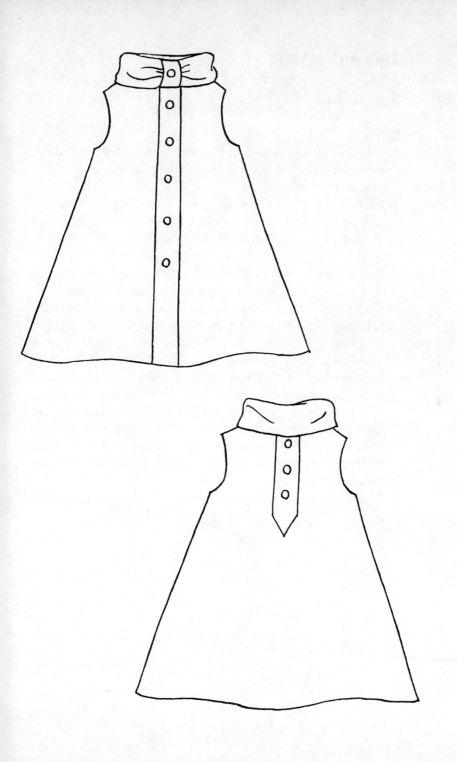

## TENT WITH SLEEVES

*materials*

same as above

*how-to*

1. Cut tent as shown above. Cut sleeves from leftover fabric, following sketch 1 (or use any sleeve pattern piece from a commercial pattern).
2. Make Basic Tent, following instructions 2 to 8 above.
3. Try on. Shoulder edges should overhang the edges of your shoulder by ⅝″. This is the seam allowance. If necessary, trim to even off shoulders.
4. Sew ribbon lace to bottom of sleeve. Fold up hem of sleeve and sew. Sew sleeve seam; iron seam open if desired.
5. To insert sleeve: Turn sleeve right side out. Turn tent wrong side out. Slip sleeve into garment so that sleeve seam meets side seam, and center top of sleeve meets outer edge of shoulder seam. Pin at these two points. Cap of sleeve should be fuller than shoulder of garment. Ease this extra fullness around, pinning every inch or so. Have more fullness near top of sleeve cap, less near underarm. With inside of sleeve facing you, sew sleeve to garment, starting at underarm and keeping ⅝″ seam allowance all around. For extra strength, sew around twice. Remove pins, of course, as you come to them.
6. Finish and trim tent as in instruction 10 above, or as desired.

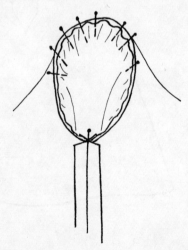

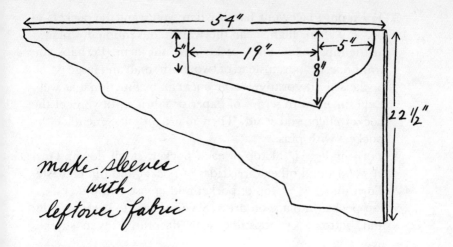

make sleeves
with
leftover fabric

## PATCH-POCKETED TENT

*materials*
same as in Basic Tent

*how-to*

1. Cut tent as shown in basic instructions above, with or without sleeves. Cut pockets from leftover fabric or contrasting fabric as shown.
2. Make the tent, sleeveless or with sleeves, following instructions above.

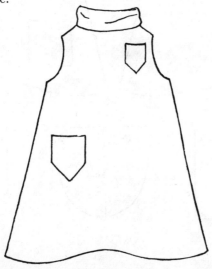

3. Try it on. Place your hands where you want the pockets to be. Try them high, near the waist, conventionally placed at the hip, or low and outside near the hem. Perhaps you want one, or four, instead of two. Both small and large patch pockets are decorative; large ones can be functional as well. Experiment with scraps of paper or fabric until you get the pocket effect you want. Then mark the placement of the pockets with pins.
4. Turn under ¼″ at top of each pocket; stitch down. Turn in ¼″ around other three sides of pocket and pin or baste. Turn under 1″ at top of pocket and crease and pin.
5. Pin pocket in place on dress. Sew invisibly to dress on sides and bottom. Or topstitch with decorative even stitches near edge.

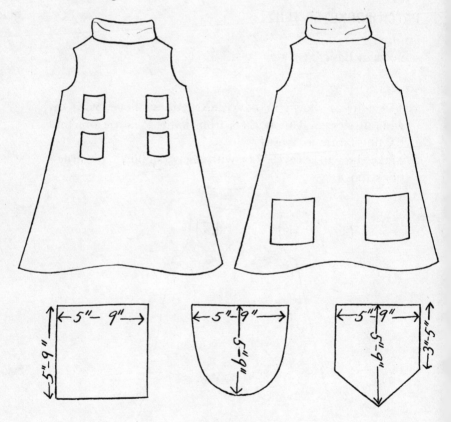

## FRONT-CLOSING TENT

*materials*

same as for Basic Tent
3 yards braid or ribbon, 1½" to 3" wide
12 to 16 silk-covered hooks and eyes

*how-to*

1. Cut as in instruction 1, above.
2. Place both back pieces together with right sides facing and sew center back seam. Do not sew front pieces together. Sew shoulder and collar seams.
3. Put tent on to fit darts. Pin together at center front, overlapping 1". Fit and pin darts as in instruction 3, Basic Tent, above.
4. Follow instructions 4 to 9 of Basic Tent, above, for sleeveless tent. For sleeved tent, follow instructions 4 to 8 of Basic Tent and 3 to 5 of Tent with Sleeves.
5. Attach braid or ribbon trim to outside right front edge. Fold ¼" raw edge of right front to *outside*; pin. Starting at inside top of hem allowance, pin trim down hem allowance, over and up outside right front, continuing trim completely up front to top of collar. Continue trim over top of collar and around to reverse of collar. Stitch trim down, catching the ¼" turned-up edge into the stitching.
6. Repeat for left front edge. Sew trim also around collar if desired.
7. Sew hooks at 3" intervals just under right front edge of tent, starting at neck and working down. Sew hooks on collar edge if desired. Sew eyes just under left front edge to correspond.
8. Add pockets if desired. Trim with same ribbon. Curved edge of collar can also be ribbon trimmed.

## LINED TENT

It will usually not be necessary to line the slipover tents, unless you want a special effect such as an outer tent of semitransparent fabric — lace or net — displaying its lining. In that case simply make two tents, one of each fabric; make the liner without the collar if you like. Slip the outer one over the inner one, and join them by sewing a few stitches invisibly through corresponding seams — at shoulders and underarms.

The Front-Closing Tent, lined, can be a coat-dress or a coat. For a coat, you might want to use an interfacing or an interlining layer between the top and lining fabrics as well. (If so, do *not* make an interfacing layer for sleeves.) Cut the lining and any other layers exactly the same as the top, and make them all up separately, following steps 1 to 6 of Basic Tent *and* step 3 of Tent with Sleeves. Sew sleeve seams. Insert sleeves as in instruction 4 of Tent with Sleeves. On outer tent

112

only turn up and sew bottom hem as in Basic Tent instruction 7. Note that sleeve hems have not been measured and sewn, and that collar has not been finished.

Put all layers together with right sides out. Pin to hold, as needed. Tack loosely together through shoulder and under-arm seams. If an interfacing or interlining is used, cut the bottom off until it is 2" or 3" shorter than bottom of outer tent. Turn lining hem allowance under so that bottom of lining is 1" to 2" shorter than outer tent. Turn hem allowance edge under ¼" and sew lining hem. Turn front and collar edges to inside, folding in ¼" all around, pinning to hold every inch or so. Stitch invisibly all around; if an interlining is used, catch the interlining in the stitching to hold it in place. Pin braid or ribbon trim along front edges and stitch as for the Front-Closing Tent. Add pockets if desired. Sew snaps at 3" intervals down front, starting at neck. Hooks and eyes set in the collar edge will allow you to wear it high or rolled if you like. For a dress or coat-dress, continue snaps down to hem; for a coat, snaps should end at or just below the hip.

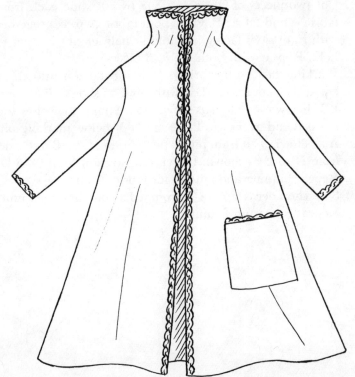

# Basic Style #10: DRAWSTRING DRESS

This easy-to-wear little dress has a wide neckline and a drawstring at the waist to let you nip it in as much or as little as you like. Choose a high Empire look, or a conventional waist, or even a low blouson effect. I have made it in a bright flower print on vinyl fabric; it is a good style for a flexible plastic cloth. But it would be equally good in piqué or broadcloth, denim or gingham, corduroy or terry, jersey or velour. With only two main seams, it is quickly put together. Make it lined or reversible; the process is practically the same.

## LINED DRAWSTRING DRESS

*materials*

2½ yards each 36″ fabric A and fabric B

*how-to*

1. Cut two pieces of fabric 45″ long by 30″ wide each from fabric A and fabric B. Place both fabric A pieces together with right sides facing and fold in half lengthwise; pin to hold. Repeat with both fabric B pieces.
2. Working first with fabric A unit, divide top into three equal 5″ sections, marked with pins, as shown. Place pin B 3″ below top at fold as shown. Place pin E 11″ below top at open end as shown. Place pin D 3″ below marking pin A as shown. Cut from pin to pin, curving from B to C and from D to E as shown, but cutting straight from C to D. Repeat pinning and cutting for fabric B unit.
3. Sew shoulder seams ½″ from edge on fabric A unit. Repeat for fabric B unit.

114

4. Try fabric A unit on. Shape darts, pinning from fullest part of bust out to side below armhole. Sew darts. Trim excess fabric from seam allowance. Repeat dart shaping for fabric B unit.

5. Sew side seams of fabric A unit. Sew side seams of fabric B unit.

6. Place fabric A unit inside fabric B unit with right sides together, wrong sides out. Sew around neckline ½″ from edge. Clip neckline seam allowance in a few places.

7. Turn right side out by pushing fabric B unit through head opening. Use fingers to smooth and even out all seams; hold A and B units together at seams with a few pins.

8. Try on dress. Determine where you want the bottom of waistband casing to be, and mark with pins. Measure up 1½″ from bottom waistband mark, and place a second row of pins to mark top of waistband casing.

9. Make waistband casing: stitch completely around dress on top and bottom waistband casing lines, sewing through both layers of fabric.

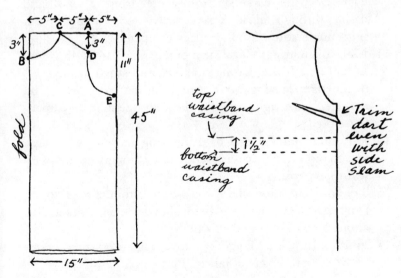

115

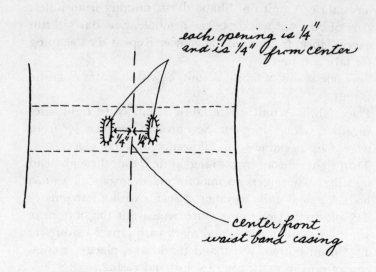

*each opening is ¼" and is ¼" from center*

*center front waist band casing*

10. Using a small sharp scissors, make two vertical openings, each ¼" wide, each ¼" from center front of waistband casing through fabric A layer only. See drawing. Work buttonhole stitch around edges of openings.

11. Make drawstring: Cut a strip of fabric A 2½" x 45". Fold in half lengthwise, wrong side out, and stitch around ¼" from edge, leaving an opening in the long side. Clip corners. Turn right side out through opening; sew opening closed.

12. Use safety pin on end of drawstring to pull it through waistband casing, leaving ends out through openings in waistband casing.

13. Try on. Determine where you want bottom of dress to be; mark hem length. Trim hem allowance if necessary to about 3". Fold up and sew hem.

14. Finish armholes: Turn ½" raw edge of armholes in, between both layers of fabric. Pin; stitch invisibly.

116

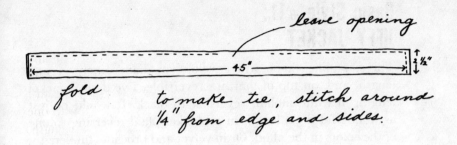

*leave opening*

45"  ↑½"

*fold*

*to make tie, stitch around ¼" from edge and sides.*

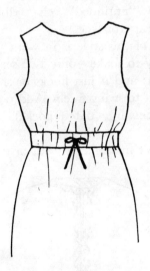

## REVERSIBLE DRAWSTRING DRESS

Make opening for drawstring on fabric B side of waistband casing as well as on fabric A side; finish in buttonhole stitch. To wear on fabric B side, pull drawstring through. Turn up hem on fabric B side and stitch invisibly, so it serves as a border matching the drawstring.

117

# Basic Style #11:
# JIFFY JACKET

This cape-like shape will envelop you handsomely in any length, and, on top of that, it's reversible. I've done it jacket length, in white mohair reversing to black. It would be just as wonderful dress length in a blanket plaid reversing to one of the colors in the plaid. Or in velvet and brocade, full length, for evening. Or combine poplin and corduroy, denim and terry cloth, or just about any fabrics you can think of. Trimming is important; it can be fine upholstery braid or rough-hewn yarn braid; "antiqued" velvet ribbon (see Part VI), serviceable grosgrain, or lace.

The flexibility of this style is in what you make of it. It's unbelievably easy to make—only two seams; the sleeves are cut on, not set in; and it just hooks or snaps up the middle, unless you want it to swing freely. Add pockets in the seam if you like; or place large patch pockets right in front over your hips.

This Jiffy Jacket makes a suit out of the Jiffy Skirt (Basic Style #4).

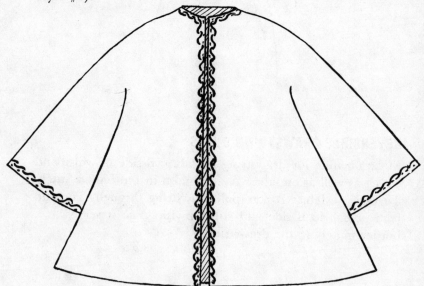

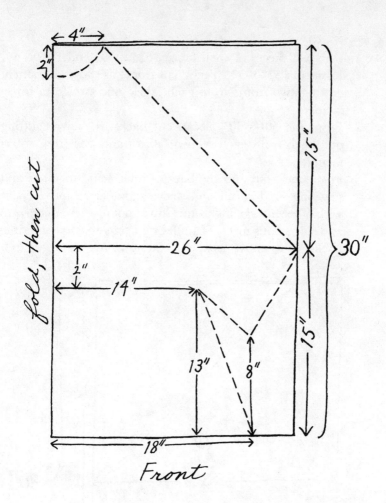

**JIFFY JACKET**

*materials*

3 yards each of two 36" fabrics
same amount interfacing
4 to 6 yards each of two braids, ribbons, or other trimmings
hooks and eyes or a silk-covered snap (optional)

1. Cut two pieces of each fabric, 52″ x 30″ and 50″ x 30″. From the 52″-x-30″ pieces, cut fronts as shown in sketch, cutting two fronts from each fabric and two from interfacing.

2. From the 50″-x-30″ pieces, cut backs as shown, cutting one back from each of two fabrics and one from interfacing.

3. Place one front and the back of interfacing together and sew side, underarm, and sleeve shoulder seams. Repeat with other interfacing front. Clip at point where underarm and side seams meet. Seam fabric fronts to corresponding backs. Press all seams open. You now have three "coats."

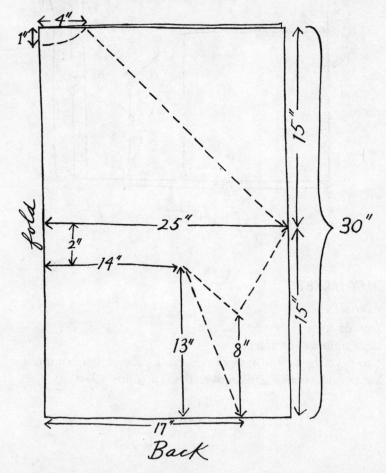

Back

clip
here

*side seam*

*underarm seam*

4. Place the three "coats" together as shown, having the two fabric layers *right sides facing* and the interfacing lying against the *wrong side* of one fabric layer. Pin at top, middle, and bottom of the four sewn seams to hold together; pin also along fronts, and at neckline if necessary.

5. Starting at bottom of front, sew up through all three layers 5/8" from edge; end stitching 5/8" from top. Repeat for second front edge.

*interfacing*

*fabric A*

*fabric B*

*wrong side out*

*right sides together*

*Cross-section*

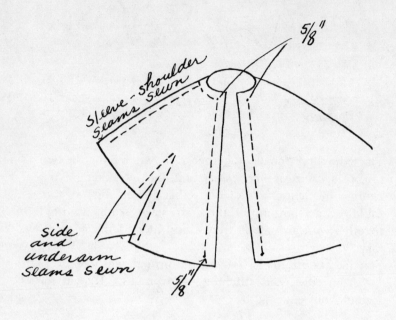

6. Sew around neckline, ⅝″ from edge, starting and ending neckline row of stitching at ends of front rows of stitching as shown. Clip corners. Trim neckline seam allowance to ¼″. Clip remaining neckline seam allowance in 6 or 8 places as shown.
7. Turn so that right sides of both fabrics are out, and interfacing is between. Roll seams between fingers to straighten. Use the point of a needle or hat pin to pull out the two corners of the neckline.
8. Turn 1″ hem allowance at bottom of sleeves to inside; stitch invisibly at bottom edge.

9. Turn 2″ to 3″ hem allowance at bottom of coat to inside (or to length desired); stitch invisibly.

10. Pin braid or other trim completely around front, neckline, and bottom of each side of jacket, just to cover edge; stitch down.

11. Sew hooks and eyes in front edges at neck, at intervals down fronts, if desired. Or sew a single silk-covered snap at front neck edge; camouflage with a small bow made of braid.

clip corners

trim and clip

front row of stitching

sleeve and shoulder seams

end neckline stitching here

start neckline stitching here

# JIFFY COAT

*materials*

3 yards each of two 42″ to 45″ fabrics
same amount interfacing
5 to 7 yards each of two braids, ribbons, or other trimmings
hooks and eyes or a silk-covered snap (optional)

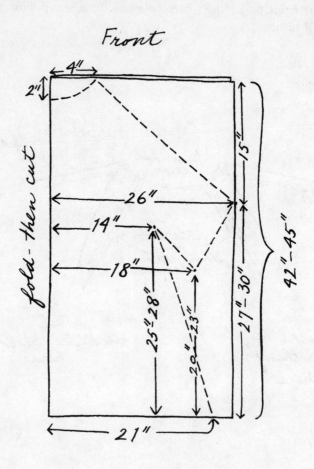

Front

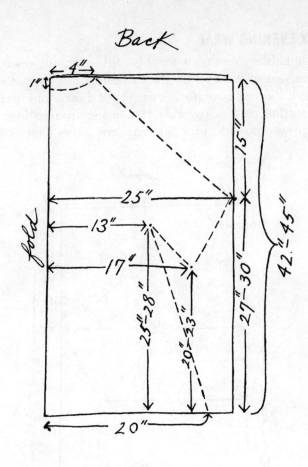

Back

*how-to*

Same as for basic Jiffy Jacket, but cut according to these diagrams.

125

## JIFFY EVENING WRAP

Use upholstery remnants for this — brocades, cut velvets — for a luxurious effect, and for the extra-long fabrics that will be needed. Piece the interfacing to get the dimensions necessary; (see section on piecing, Part II); or use iron-on interfacing and press onto one fabric after pattern pieces have been cut.

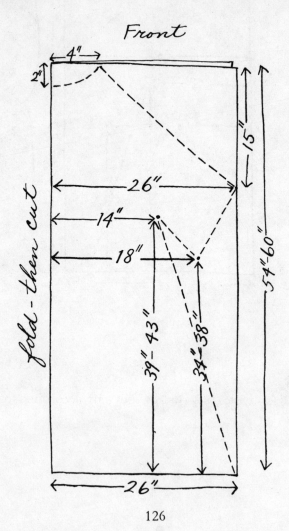

Front

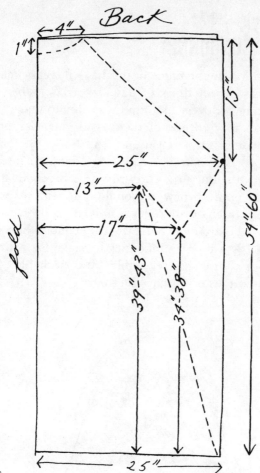

*materials*

3 yards each of two 54″ to 60″ fabrics
same amount interfacing
6 to 8 yards of two braids, ribbons, or other trimmings
hooks and eyes or a silk-covered snap (optional)

*how-to*

Same as for basic Jiffy Jacket, but follow these diagrams for
cutting pattern pieces.

127

# Basic Style #12:
# QUAKER SUNBONNET

Don't be misled by the name of this hat—it wears beautifully in all seasons, at all times of day. It makes a becomingly feminine frame for every face, and is so easy to make that you can whip up a wardrobe of them. Did you ever hear of a tweed sunbonnet? Or a velvet one? Just try it. Of course you can use all sorts of cottons—calico, bandanna-printed cloth, denim, sailcloth. But in a corduroy or a brocade, this style takes on an entirely new personality; it will surprise and delight you. Match one to every suit, coat, or dress you make —an extra half-yard or so of fabric will be more than enough.

Oh, yes. It's a lovely sunbonnet to make for a little girl, too. And, of course, it's reversible. And packable. Just un-button the buttons or unsnap the snaps.

*Quaker Sun Bonnet*

## QUAKER SUNBONNET

*materials*

½ yard each of two fabrics
same amount of interfacing
2″ strip of elastic, ¼″ wide
9 silk-covered snaps (or 9 buttons)

*how-to*

1. Follow layout sketch 1a if you have one piece of fabric;
   otherwise, cut pieces 18″ x 8″ (A) and 14″ x 14″ (B) and
   two long pieces 2″ wide and 18″ to 24″ long. Cut pieces A
   and B only from interfacing. Follow sketches 1b to cut the
   brim and crown.

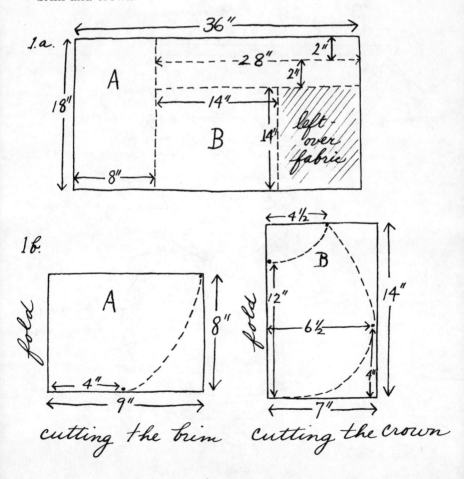

1.a.

left over fabric

1b.

cutting the brim     cutting the crown

2. Place all brims together so that right sides of both fabrics are together and interfacing and wrong side of one fabric are on outside. Stitch around, leaving three openings, as shown. Clip seam allowance on curved side in several places; cut off corners as shown. Turn right sides out through opening in straight edge. Close up this opening.

3. Place the crown piece of interfacing on the wrong side of one of the fabric crown pieces. Pin at corners to hold in place. Center strip of elastic on edge of interfacing between pins; place pin through center as shown. With elastic facing you, sew from this pin out, pulling the elastic as you sew. Sew from center out to other end of elastic, pulling elastic as before.

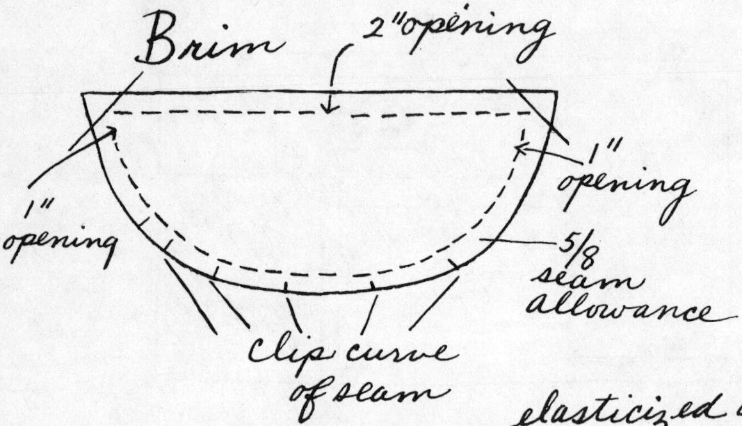

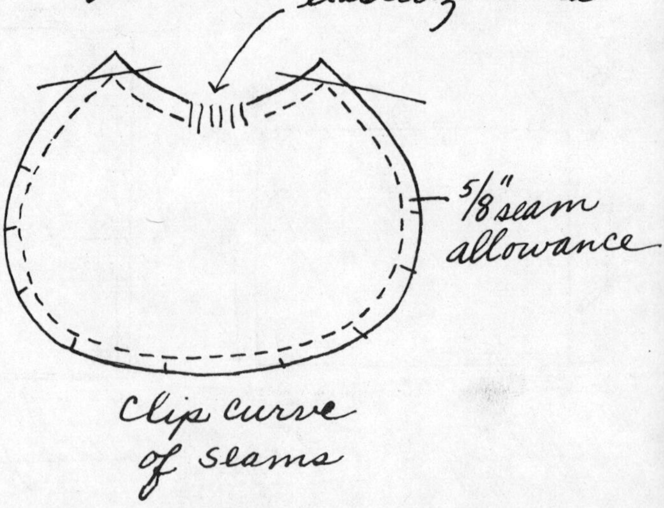

Brim    2" opening

1" opening

1" opening

5/8 seam allowance

Clip curve of seam

elasticized area

5/8" seam allowance

Clip curve of seams

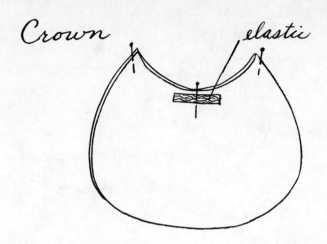

*Crown*     *elastic*

4. Place crown piece with elastic on other fabric crown piece so that right sides of both fabrics are together and interfacing and wrong side of one fabric are on outside. Pin at corners. Sew around as shown, leaving elasticized area open. Clip seam allowance on curve as shown; cut off corners. Turn right sides out through opening; sew up opening.

5. To make ties, put two different fabrics right sides together. Cut a triangular piece off one corner as shown. Sew around tie piece, down one long side, across angle, and up other long side, ¼″ from edge; leave short end open. Clip point as shown. Turn tie right side out, pushing point through opening at opposite end with the blunt end of a knitting needle or a pencil. Repeat for other tie.

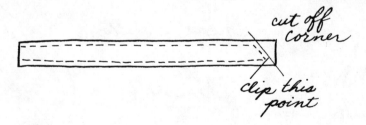

*cut off corner*

*clip this point*

# Crown

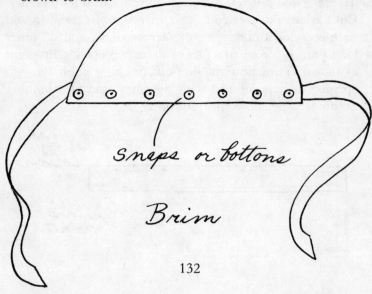

snaps or
button holes

6. Gather open ends of ties to fit 1″ openings in sides of brim. Pin in place; sew down, closing openings and firmly attaching ties.

7. Sew 9 snaps (or buttons) at evenly spaced intervals across straight edge of brim, as shown. (To make reversible, sew snaps or buttons on both sides, sewing through one layer of fabric only.) Sew remaining parts of snaps (or make buttonholes) around crown, as shown. Snap or button crown to brim.

snaps or bottons

Brim

## LITTLE GIRL'S BONNET

To make this for a youngster, cut the crown and brim to the dimensions shown. The ties should be 18" long. Use 7 snaps or buttons instead of 9. Follow directions as before.

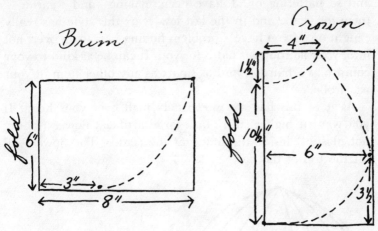

## INFANT'S BONNET

Cut crown and brim to dimensions shown. Make ties 12" long. Use 7 silk-covered snaps or small buttons. Follow directions as before.

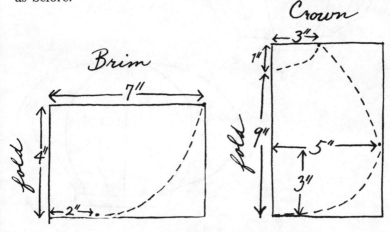

# Basic Style #13: CHEF'S HAT

Here is another wonderful hat, soft and crushable off the head and so flattering on. I have been making — and wearing — them for years, and in the last few years this style has really caught on. If you have a problem finding hats to go over, not into, your hairdo, this hat is for you. It can be as kind to your coiffure as a hairnet; and as smart as any other item in your wardrobe.

As it is, this hat sits moderately high over your head. If you want it higher still, pin a large artificial flower (fabric, not plastic!) inside the lining at the center. The flower will lift the top of the hat.

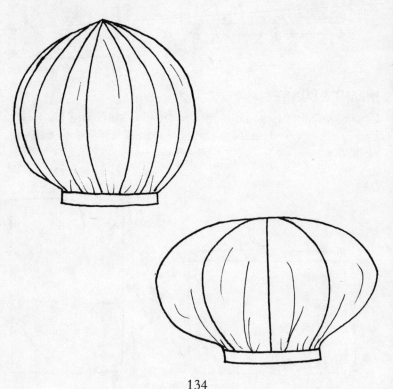

## CHEF'S HAT

*materials*

½ yard (or less) of any fabric—enough to give 8 pieces of fabric 5″ x 9″ *or* 16 pieces of fabric 3″ x 10″. (Scraps left over from other garments; the piece cut off a hem when shortening a dress, coat, or suit; or different patterned pieces from your "ragbag" will be fine; just make sure that pieces used are of approximately the same weight.)

½ yard interfacing (if fabric for hat is lightweight—i.e., silk, sheer wool, soft cotton)

½ yard of fabric for lining (Odd pieces may be used here, too; but they should be of the same light weight; an old silk kerchief might serve.)

for headband, a strip of ribbon, fabric, or colored, soft elastic 2″ or 2½″ wide and long enough to go around your head plus 1″

a button form, a decorative button, or a large bead

*how-to*

1. Cut 8 pieces of fabric to the dimensions shown in 1*a*, or 16 pieces of fabric to the dimensions shown in 1*b* (if you are working with very small strips of fabric, 1*b* will be your choice). Repeat with interfacing, if used. Repeat with

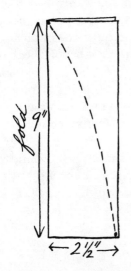
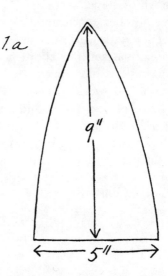

1.*a*

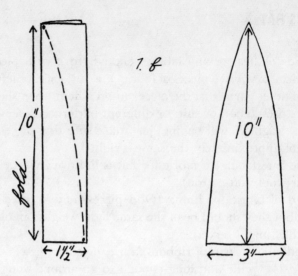

lining fabric. Note that cut pieces are triangles whose identical sides curve slightly outward.

2. If interfacing is used, match one section of interfacing to the wrong side of a section of the hat fabric. Sew around ¼″ from edge.

3. Place two sections of hat fabric right sides together and sew down one side, keeping a ⅜″ seam allowance and starting the stitches ⅜″ from the point. Open up; place another section with its right side facing the right side of one of the already-attached sections, and sew together. Repeat until all sections have been attached. Sew the last remaining seam. Still working on the wrong side, hold all pieces together at the point and sew the point opening closed, working back and forth with the sewing machine.

4. Repeat with lining sections.

5. Cut headband to fit your head: measure *loosely* around your head and add 1″. Cut strip of fabric 2″ or 2½″ wide — matching or contrasting — or ribbon to this length. Fold in

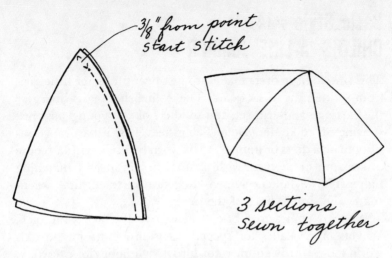

3/8" from point
start stitch

3 sections
sewn together

half lengthwise, right side out, and press a soft crease with iron or damp fingers. Fold in half crosswise, right side in, and sew ends together ½" from edge.

6. Place right side of headband against right side of hat, with edges meeting, and pin in 4 places. Work fullness of hat evenly into headband, pinning around as necessary. Stitch ½" from edge; run another row of stitching just outside the first for extra strength.

7. Fold headband on crease made in step 5. Place lining inside hat. Turn lining edges in and stitch over free edge of headband. (Cover this row of stitching with ribbon lace if desired.)

8. Cover a button form with the same fabric. Sew over point. Or sew a decorative button or large bead over point.

*Note:* An elastic headband, or one made of a stretch fabric, will let the hat go easily over an elaborate hairdo. When sewing any elastic or stretch fabric, stretch it out as taut as possible as you stitch.

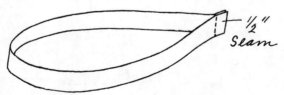

½"
seam

# Basic Style #14:
# CHILD'S A-LINE JUMPER

This simple little dress makes up just beautifully for little girls from six months to six years. The A-line shaping is smart for the carriage-and-crib set, the toddler, or the young miss just starting off to kindergarten. Being sleeveless, it has the versatility to be a dress or jumper, to be worn by itself, with a blouse or sweater, or perhaps with a turtle-neck top and matching tights. The keyhole neckline is a decorative touch that accentuates the simple lines of the dress.

When it comes to fabric, you can really take your pick. Velvets or brocades for special occasions; knits for an old-world look; sturdy cottons, corduroys, synthetics for everyday. Trim with bias binding, grosgrain or velvet ribbon, satin lace, wool braid, eyelet lace. Make a party dress in plum velvet with pale blue lace trim; a denim country dress with red-and-white checked trim.

Add a lining for an extra-special touch, and practicality, too. If you line the dress as though you were making it reversible, there will be a hidden hem of fresh fabric to let down next year, for added wear. Add a pocket, and tie a bow on it to match the bow at the neckline. Some little girl will be delighted.

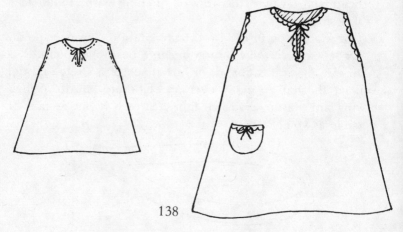

138

|  | infant 6 mos. – 1 yr. | toddler 2 – 4 yrs. | little girl 4 – 6 yrs. |
|---|---|---|---|
| A – B (back) | ½" | ¾" | 1" |
| A – B' (front) | 1 ½" | 1 ¾" | 2" |
| A – C | 11" | 15" | 19" |
| A – D | 2 ½" | 2 ¾" | 3" |
| B – E | 5" | 5 ½" | 6" |
| D – F | 2 ½" | 2 ¾" | 3" |
| E – F | ½" | ¾" | 1" |
| H – G | 10" | 12" | 14" |

*materials*

1 yard 39" fabric
1 yard 39" fabric for lining
2 yards lace, ribbon, bias or other trim

*how-to*

1. Cut 1 front and 1 back each from top fabric and from lining as in sketch, following measurements in chart according to size.

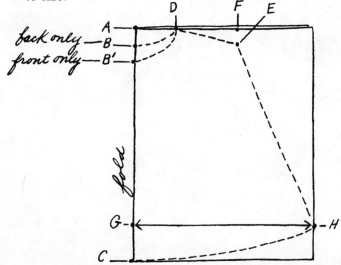

2. At center top of *front pieces only*, slash down 3″ (3½″; 4″) for neck opening.
3. Place front and back of dress with right sides together and sew up side seams, starting from bottom and working to within 5″ (5½″; 6″) of top; this will be armhole. Sew shoulder seams.
4. Repeat with lining.
5. Place lining inside dress, right sides out. Pin to hold at shoulder seams and in side seams. Turn ½″ to inside at neckline and armhole openings; pin all around. Stitch down; machine stitching close to edges may be used, as neckline and armholes will be covered with decorative trim.
6. Turn up hem: turn 2″ or whatever hem allowance is needed to inside (between outside and lining fabrics) at bottom. Pin; sew invisibly with light stitches. *Do not iron!* Just smooth with your fingers, over and over again if necessary, until bottom edge of dress is smooth. Your light stitches will never leave a mark, and your unpressed hem will never tell tales when you lengthen this dress next year!
7. Pin trimming around neckline and armholes. Sew down. Cut two 10″ strips of your trimming and stitch to front corners of neckline for ties; free ends may be knotted to prevent raveling.

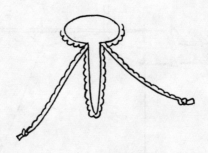

## JUMPER WITH POCKET(S)

*materials*

same fabric requirements as above; pocket is cut from left-over pieces

an extra ½ yard of trimming

*how-to*

1. Follow steps 1 to 3 above.
2. For each pocket, cut one each from top and lining fabric as shown in diagram.
3. Place top and lining pocket pieces together with right sides facing and sew all around ½" from edge, leaving an opening at the bottom. Turn right sides out through this opening. Sew opening closed.
4. Fold pocket in half lengthwise and mark center top with a pin. Pin 4 tucks on each side of center. Tack down.
5. Pin trimming along top of pocket; stitch down. Make a small bow out of trimming and stitch to center of pocket.
6. Place pocket where desired on dress; pin. Sew in place.
7. Finish dress, following steps 3 to 7 above.

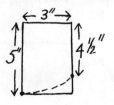

## JUMPER WITH DRAWSTRING NECKLINE

This variation is made somewhat differently, but the basic lines of the dress are the same. It can be done without the lining for real speed; and the velvet ribbon that ties demurely at each shoulder is all the trimming it needs. One or two pockets may be added, following instructions above, if desired.

*materials*

1 yard 39″ fabric
1½ yards ¼″ velvet or other ribbon
3 yards ¼″ ribbon lace

*how-to*

1. Cut both front and back as in diagram, referring to chart for measurements according to size.
2. Attach ribbon lace to both side edges of each piece; this will be the seam finishing and the armhole facing.
3. Place both pieces together with right sides facing and sew ½″ side seams, stitching from hem to within 5½″ (6″; 6½″) of top. Hem down ribbon lace to finish armhole edges.
4. On front, turn ½″ under on wrong side twice at neck edge; hem down. Repeat for back. This forms the casing for the drawstring.

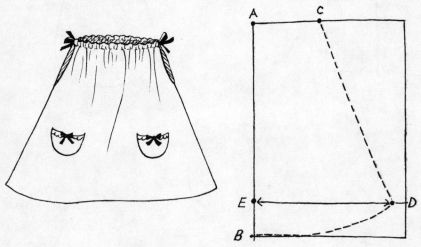

|       | infant 6 mos. - 1 yr. | toddler 2 - 4 | little girl 4 - 6 |
| --- | --- | --- | --- |
| A-B | 11" | 15" | 19" |
| A-C | 4½" | 5" | 5½" |
| D-E | 10" | 12" | 14" |

5. Attach ribbon lace to bottom edge of jumper. Turn up 2" to 3" or whatever is necessary for hem. Sew hem.
6. Cut ribbon in half. Starting at one open end, use safety pin to pull one piece through front casing and around through back casing. Start at the opposite open end with the other piece of ribbon and pull through front and back casings in the other direction. Each ribbon will then have its two ends on the same side to go over one shoulder, and to act as a drawstring. Shirr casing gently with fingers and tie little bows at each shoulder. Cut ends of ribbons off at angle.

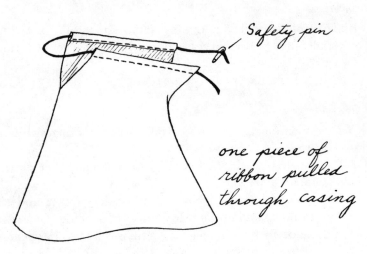

Safety pin

one piece of ribbon pulled through casing

143

# Basic Style #15:
# RUFFLED BONNET

This little hat is great for the baby or girl who will get one of the A-Line Jumpers (Basic Style #14). Make it to match, of leftover pieces of fabric. Or to match anything else. Or make it out of crisp white pique lined with blue or pink or yellow or orange to shade a tiny head on a summer's day.

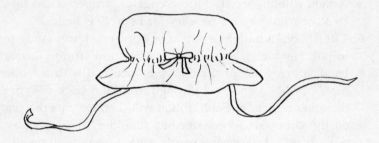

*materials*

2 pieces of fabric 15″ x 15″ for infant size or 17″ x 17″ for toddler size (fabric pieces may be the same or contrasting)

½ yard ¼″ elastic

1 yard ¼″ ribbon

*how-to*

*Note:* dimensions given are for infant size; toddler size is in parentheses.

1. Cut two fabric circles 15″ (17″) in diameter. (See cutting directions, Part II.)
2. Place both pieces together with right sides facing and sew ½″ from edge all around, leaving a 2″ opening. Clip seam allowance in several places. Turn through this opening.

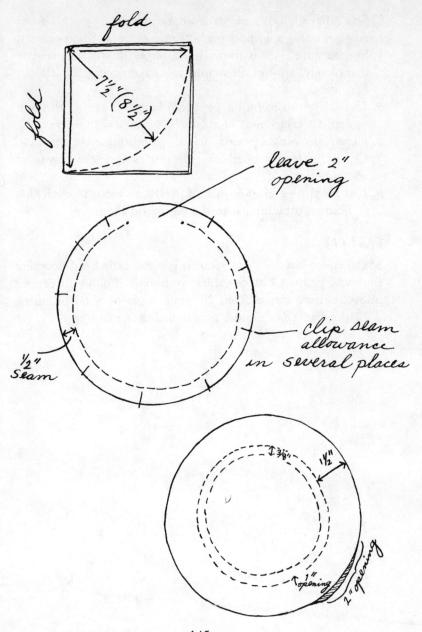

fold

fold

$7\frac{1}{2}$" ($8\frac{1}{2}$")

leave 2"
opening

clip seam
allowance
in several places

$\frac{1}{2}$"
Seam

$1\frac{3}{8}$"

$1\frac{1}{2}$"

1" opening

2" opening

145

3. Sew through both pieces from right side 1½″ (2″) from edge, leaving a 1″ opening at same place as first opening.
4. Sew around ⅜″ in from the last row of stitches, sewing completely around this time to make casing for elastic. See sketch.
5. Use safety pin to pull a 14″ (18″) length of elastic through casing. Overlap ends of elastic ¼″ and sew together.
6. Close up casing opening. Close up outside edge opening.
7. Cut a 10″ length of ribbon; tie into a bow. Sew on front of bonnet.
8. Cut remaining ribbon in half. Sew one piece to each side of bonnet, attaching it to the casing on the inside.

## BABY CAP

Make yourself a baby cap, too. It is a soft little head covering that will protect but not muss your hair. Follow directions above, cutting circles from 20″ square pieces of fabric, using a 22″ long piece of elastic, and omitting ties in step 8.

# IV

# Transformations

In this section I am going to show you how to convert used, outdated items into new, glamorous garments; how to take things that are ready for the ragbag and transform them into useful, attractive clothes; or simply how to make some inexpensive, everyday items into one-of-a-kind conversation pieces. Two old skirts will combine to make one new one. Everybody's old poplin raincoat becomes a versatile and stunning wear-anytime Sunny Day Coat. A pair of pettipants turns into party pants. A worn-out man's shirt becomes a pants top or a smock-dress. Dungarees get a dress-up treatment. And much, much more.

But even more important than these ideas and step-by-step instructions are the ideas you yourself will get for transforming the tired items in your own bureau or closet. Next time you go through your things to see what you can discard, change your approach: see what you can *rescue!* Try looking at things with an objective, free eye: you are a designer working on the problem of using something old as the starting point for something new. You will appreciate, perhaps for the first time, the lines of an old sweater or robe, the fabric in an old slip or dress, the possibilities in a jacket if only its sleeves and collar were removed or changed. You will be surprised to discover that almost everything — things you would normally throw or give away — will give you an inspiration for a new design.

147

# Transformation #1:
# MAN'S OR BOY'S SWEATER WITH BUILT-IN TIE AND COLLAR

*stitch ribbon over raw edge of shirt collar*

With this sweater on, he will be able to go into any restaurant and no one will know he isn't really wearing a shirt and tie.

*materials*

1 old sweater (crew-neck pullover style)
1 old necktie, tied
2 matching button-down collars (removed from man's shirts —see Transformations #2 and #3 for uses for shirts with collars removed)
2 collar buttons
½ yard ½" grosgrain ribbon

*how-to*

1. Mark center front of sweater neckline with pin. Starting ½" on either side of marking pin, pin each collar to neckline. Fit fold of collar over neck edge, stretching knit out. Allow for ½" overlap where collars meet at center back of neckline; cut excess off both collars. Pin ½" seam at center back.
2. Stitch collars down to sweater, sewing from wrong side through sweater to catch outside of collar invisibly. Don't worry about any raw edges of collar on the wrong side: they will be covered with ribbon later on.

148

3. Tie necktie. Stitch knot securely in place, sewing from underside. Cut off extra tie fabric, leaving 1½" on each side of knot. Cut off back length just below knot. Stitch these three cut edges just enough to keep from raveling.
4. Place tie in position between collar points on sweater. Pin. Stitch down invisibly.
5. Sew collar buttons underneath buttonholes on collar points.
6. Place ribbon over raw edge of collar and stitching on wrong side of sweater and sew invisibly in place.

# Transformation #2:
# BABY DRESS (FOR BABY, LITTLE GIRL, OR BIG GIRL) FROM BOY'S OR MAN'S SHIRT

No one would ever believe that such a feminine style started life as a boy's or man's shirt.

In its new guise it buttons down the back, and will fit girls of any size, depending on the size of the shirt it is made from. A little boy's shirt, sizes 4-6, makes a baby dress or top for a baby. A man's shirt, neck size 14, makes a baby dress for a schoolgirl, size 6-8. In this size it also becomes a smock-blouse for a teenager or woman.

Actually, you control the size of this loosely fitting garment by making the elastic at the neckband looser or tighter, cutting the sleeves shorter or longer, or by turning up more or less hem allowance.

*materials*
1 boy's or man's shirt
braid or lace trim (optional)
1 yard ¼" elastic

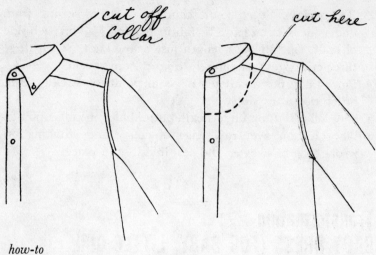

*cut off collar*

*cut here*

*how-to*

1. Cut off shirttails; pin up hem.
2. Cut off cuff or lower part of sleeve to length desired. Turn sleeve edge under ¼″ and pin. For loose sleeve, turn under again and hem. For elastic-gathered sleeve, turn under ½″ to make casing and stitch around, leaving a 1″ opening to insert elastic. Repeat for other sleeve.
3. Cut off collar; fold shirt in quarters lengthwise and cut out quarter-oval, cutting between top button and second button as shown. Turn neck edge under ⅛″; turn under ½″ more to make casing for elastic and sew, leaving ends open.
4. Pull elastic through sleeve casings; cut off excess, overlap edges, and stitch. Sew up openings in casings.
5. Pull elastic through neckline casing. Try on to get right length of elastic. Pin at each end. Cut off excess. Stitch ends of elastic to ends of neckline casing.
6. Sew hem.
7. If desired, make a pocket from one or both of the cut-off cuffs. Turn edges in and stitch in place on dress.
8. If desired, run trim (braid, rickrack, etc.) under casings to hide stitches. Use trim to outline pockets, too. Or a row of embroidery might replace the sewn-on trim.

150

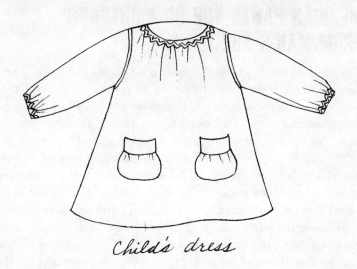

*Child's dress*

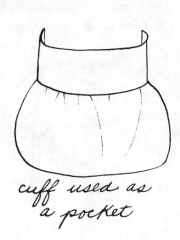

*cuff used as
a pocket*

# Transformation #3:
# MEXICAN PANTS TOP OR NIGHTSHIRT
# FROM MAN'S SHIRT

Collar and cuffs worn and frayed on a man's old shirt? Then cut them off; trim with fringe or braid for a south-of-the-border look to wear with pants, as a smock, as a beach cover-up, or even to bed. The same approach will freshen up your own tired-out man-styled shirt. The color and fabric of the shirt, and the type of decorative treatment you give it, will determine how to wear your Mexican shirt. A fine white-on-white or pastel-blue-on-white shirt, trimmed with white or pastel lace, would make a very dainty, feminine sleep smock. A yellow shirt with orange braid or fringe trim, on the other hand, could be the top of a hostess outfit. Embroidered ribbon will give a Russian peasant effect. Match your trim to the colors of your favorite bathing suit for a swinging patio dress. Buy an appliqué monogram at your notions counter; tint it any color you choose, using a teaspoonful of dye in a cup of hot water; and sew it on the pocket of your shirt.

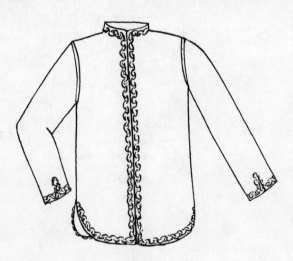

*materials*

1 old man's or man-styled shirt

3½ yards (approximately) of cotton fringe upholstery braid, ruffled lace, or any desired trim.

*how-to*

1. Cut off collar just above neckband; stitching on neckband will keep edge from raveling. Cut off cuffs; turn edge under ¼″ twice and machine stitch or hem. Sew edges of opening at bottom sleeve together. Do not cut off shirttails.
2. Cut a piece of fringe ¾″ longer than top of each pocket. Turn in edges and pin to pocket top.
3. Pin fringe around sleeve bottom and up stitched opening.
4. Pin fringe completely around shirt: up one front edge, around collar, down other front edge, and around shirt-tails. For a Mexican wedding-shirt look, pin ruffled lace in four rows on each side of the center front, covering up the pocket, for a bib effect, as shown in sketch.
5. Sew fringe, lace, or other trim in place.

This is a lovely way to transform a boy's outgrown shirt into a sophisticated topping for his little sister, too.

For a whimsical effect, use the cut-off cuffs to fashion extra pockets and place them anywhere — top, bottom, or on the sleeves.

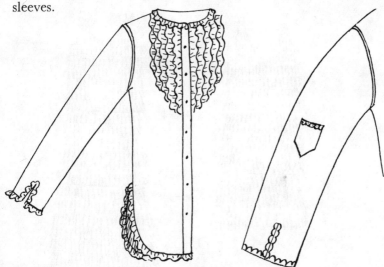

# Transformation #4:
# FRINGE SKIRT, BLOUSE, OR DRESS

A wonderful way to make a coordinated outfit from un-matched, time- or closet-worn items is to cover them with overlapping rows of decorative fringe. Short cotton fringe is inexpensive; long silk upholstery fringe is luxurious; bright yarn fringe is smartly sporty. Whichever you choose, you will have the most original new outfit in town.

There is no end to the types of outfits that can be created in this way. A simple shell and two petticoats, one cut short to tunic length, combine to make a triple-tiered cocktail dress. Change the bottom petticoat to one of evening length for a sophisticated gown. An old skirt and an odd jacket become a suit when the skirt is covered with fringe and the jacket trimmed to match. Sweaters, slacks, shifts, even robes are all candidates for this easy dress-up treatment. And don't ignore the possibilities of using overlapping layers of fringe to lengthen garments, either. Perhaps a skirt from several seasons back, with its hem let all the way down, can be given a fringe-layered border to extend it to evening or at-home length. A short-sleeved sweater or blouse can get longer, wider

154

sleeves; tapered slacks can be made wider and longer at the bottom; and a child's party dress can be given a new lease on life.

*materials*

The amount of fringe needed depends on the garment to be transformed. You will need less yardage of long fringe than you will of short fringe: to make a three-piece dress by covering a shell blouse, petticoat shortened to tunic length, and a dress-length petticoat might require 20 yards of 2″ fringe, but only 10 yards of 4″ fringe.

*how-to*

Pin fringe on garment in overlapping rows. If you want to completely cover the base color of the foundation garment, you will want fringe that has a wide braid top; and you will overlap it closely. If you would like the foundation fabric to show through, choose long fringe on a narrow top.

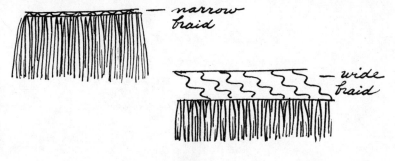

*Follow the lines* of the foundation garment. Rows of fringe should meet at the seams. Cut the fringe for each row ¾" longer than the distance from seam to seam; turn under ⅜" at each end of fringe and pin in place.

*Pin all fringe before sewing.* You will have a chance to arrange the overlapping more or less densely if it seems necessary.

When lengthening or widening a part of a garment, it may be necessary first to add a fabric layer to the original garment

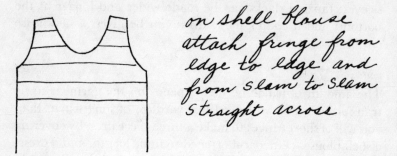

on shell blouse
attach fringe from
edge to edge and
from seam to seam
straight across

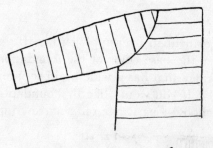

note how fringe
is turned in at
garment seams to
follow original
lines

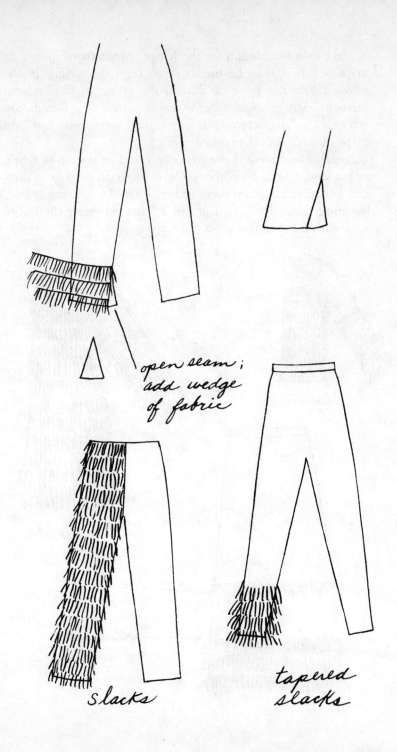

open seam;
add wedge
of fabric

slacks

tapered
slacks

to serve as a foundation for the fringe. Any leftover pieces or strips of fabric may be used; try to keep the weight of the added fabric the same as that of the fabric in the original garment. Add a strip of light-weight cotton as a foundation extension to silk, cotton, or other light garments; but add strips of wool fabric to heavier cloth.

*Lengthen* by letting down hems and adding a strip of fabric at bottom of hem allowances. Cover both original hem lines and added strip with rows of fringe. *Widen* by opening seams, inserting triangular strips of fabric, and covering the entire area with overlapping rows of fringe.

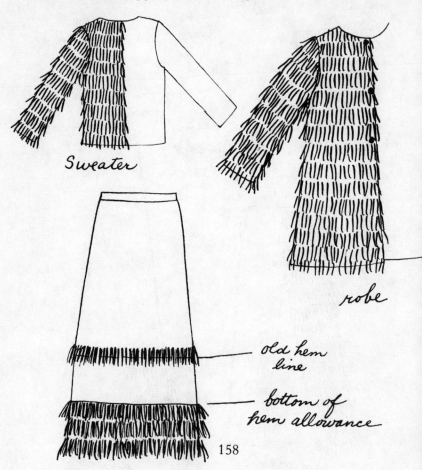

Sweater

robe

old hem line

bottom of hem allowance

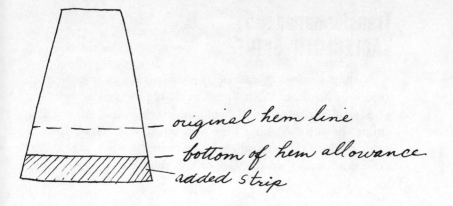

original hem line

bottom of hem allowance

added strip

short-sleeved
sweater or blouse

old hem line

bottom of hem
allowance

child's dress

159

# Transformation #5: TABLECLOTH SKIRT

A swirling circle skirt can be made from a square tablecloth in almost no time. With linens available in such a wide and wonderful range of colors, you can have a skirt of any hue under the sun. Or, next time you outfit your table, buy an extra cloth to match and make yourself a hostess skirt. Wear these skirts with a simple shell or knit shirt, trimmed to match.

*materials*

1 48″ to 54″ square tablecloth
1 yard ⅜″ elastic
3 silk-covered snaps
4 to 5 yards ball fringe

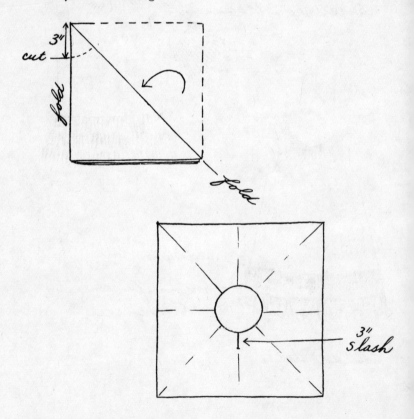

*Back of skirt,*
*untrimmed*

*how-to*

1. Fold tablecloth in quarters, then in eighths to get center. Cut wedge 3″ down from center point. Slash down 3″ from cut edge in the middle of one side, as shown, for back opening.

2. Turn cut curved edge under ¼″ and then ½″; hem to form casing for elastic waistband.

3. Cut elastic 1″ longer than waist measurement. Insert in casing, using safety pin to pull through. Pin at each side opening of casing.

4. Turn sides of back opening in ⅛″ and then ¼″; stitch, catching ends of elastic firmly in place.

5. Try skirt on. Pin at waist so that back opening edges overlap about ½″ at top. If this makes waistband too tight, have these edges just meet, instead of overlapping. Turn four corners up until skirt is desired length; pin as shown. Bottom of skirt will be gracefully uneven; and corners will make four low pockets.

161

6. If waistband is overlapped, sew on snaps, attaching one at very top near edge, one at bottom of back opening, and one in the middle, If waistband sides meet, use large hooks on right-hand side and make thread loops just under edge on wrong side of left, as shown.

7. Topstitch along one edge and bottom third of other edge of turned-up corners, as shown.

8. If desired, make a flower from circle that was cut out to form waistband: using strong or double thread, sew a ring of running stitches ½" from center of circle and gather tightly. Cut one ball off of large ball fringe, or three balls off of small ball fringe, and sew (or paste, using extra-strong white all-purpose glue) in center of gathered circle. Attach the "flower" to one of the front corner pockets. Embroider green leaves if desired.

9. Attach ball fringe around bottom of skirt.

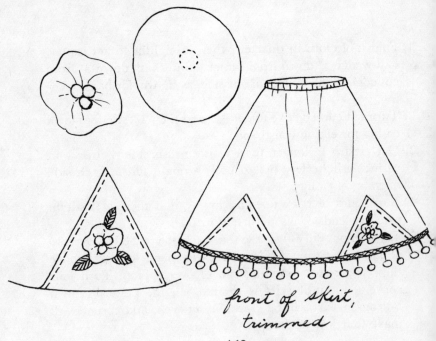

front of skirt, trimmed

# Transformation #6:
# A-LINE SKIRT FROM STRAIGHT SKIRT

In every closet there hangs a suit that is now several seasons old, but made of such lovely fabric that it can't be tossed away without twinges of guilt. It is fondled twice a year, wistfully; and then tucked away to await the unlikely day that the styles will change and we will once again wear our skirts uncomfortably pegged and long. But there is no need to wait for this day. You can enjoy your old skirt now, with the skirt eased up and shortened to today's new casually comfortable look. Here's how to change

this          to this:

*materials*

1 straight skirt

extra fabric: this may be located in the old hem allowance of the skirt; in the sleeves of its matching jacket; in a coordinated blouse; or any contrasting fabric of approximately the same weight (another skirt would be fine, too)

· 163

1. Open side seams of skirt to 1″ below waistband. Remove side zipper if there is one. Try on. If waist is too tight open hook or button and mark new waist closing with a pin. Mark new hem at desired length. Leave a 2″ or 3″ hem allowance and cut off any excess. (If you will use the old hem allowance to transform your skirt, leave only 1″ hem allowance; you will later attach a 2″ wide piece of ribbon as a hem-allowance extender.)

2. Measure distance from cut edge of hem allowance to bottom of waistband. You have to cut 4 right triangles whose longer straight sides are this length. Lay them out on your extra fabric in one of the ways shown below. Note that the shorter straight side of the triangle may be of any length, from 3″ to 6″; if you have enough extra fabric, by all means make it 6″; but do not worry if you only have enough fabric to get a 3 piece. (Even 2½″ might be enough to transform your skirt; if that's all you have, try it anyway. If it still seems too scanty to you, try adding a strip of grosgrain ribbon in the necessary additional width to the long straight side of

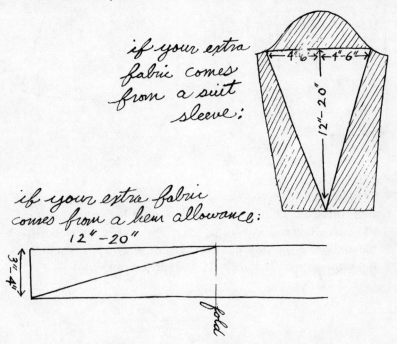

*if your extra fabric comes from a suit sleeve:*

4″-6″  4″-6″

12″-20″

*if your extra fabric comes from a hem allowance:*

12″-20″

3″-4″

*fold*

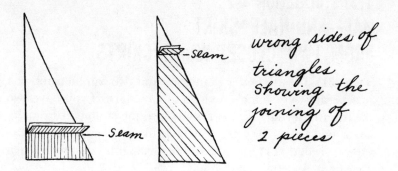

seam

seam

wrong sides of triangles showing the joining of 2 pieces

the triangle.) It may be helpful to cut one or several patterns from paper in order to get the best layout of the widest triangle from your fabric.

It will probably be necessary to add to the length of the triangles; if so, use other scraps, such as the shaded areas in the sketch showing how to lay out the triangles on a sleeve. If there is no other fabric available, simply use as much length as you have, and set in your triangles from 4″ to 8″ below the waistband, as necessary. When adding fabric to the triangle, add it on in straight horizontal rows, either at the top or at the bottom, as shown. Make a ¼″ seam to join the pieces.

3. Place the straight side of each triangle against a seam side of the original skirt, right sides facing. Pin; seam.
4. Seam the diagonal sides of the two triangles on each side of the skirt together.
5. If there was a side zipper on the skirt, reset it into the new left skirt seam.
6. If necessary, alter the waistline as marked in step 1.
7. If your hem allowance needs to be extended, now is the time to add a 2″ wide length of ribbon to it; sew ribbon on as you would any seam binding. Otherwise, sew ribbon lace or seam binding to edge of hem allowance. Turn up hem allowance as marked previously; hem.

# Transformation #7:
# HALF-AND-HALF SKIRT
# FROM TWO CLOSET-WORN SKIRTS

Two old skirts are better than one. And two can be combined in several ways, to make one great new skirt. If you have two skirts with, let us say, worn seats, use the still-good fronts to get a two-tone skirt that will look like the drawings below. Or the second skirt can provide the triangular wedges to turn a straight skirt into an A-line.

*materials*
2 old skirts, of approximately the same weight fabric

*how-to*
1. Decide which of the above possibilities best suits the good portions of the skirts with which you are working. Then follow direction 2 for the first skirt or direction 3 for the second.
2. Open hems of both skirts. Open side seams up to waistband; if there is a side zipper, leave it attached at the left seam of the new skirt front. Leave waistband tab attached. Leave skirt fronts attached to waistband; open waistband seams on *old skirt backs only*, for ¾″ beyond side seam. Cut here. You now have two skirt pieces that look like this: Place together with right sides facing and pin along side seam edges, starting from just below waistband and continuing down to bottom. Turn right side out; try on. Determine

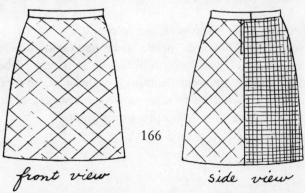

166

*front view*          *side view*

hem length desired; mark with pin. Cut off excess fabric 2″ to 3″ below new hemline. Sew new side seams; attach zipper to seam allowance at left back. Pin waistband seam; sew. Sew ribbon lace (or seam binding) to bottom edge of hem allowance. Hem. Sew snaps or hooks and eyes on to waistband tabs.

3. Open hems of both skirts. Fold skirt to be cut through center front and center back, matching side seams, and pin together. Measure side seam of other skirt from bottom of hem allowance to just under waistband, if skirt has back closing; to just under zipper if skirt has side closing. Measure this length off on side seam of skirt to be cut; mark with pin. Determine desired width of triangular addition—say, 6″ —and measure this off on either side of side seam of skirt to be cut. Use ruler to mark with pins a straight line tapering from this width at the bottom to a point at the pin marking the top of the addition. See sketch. Cut through both layers of skirt to just under waistband or to just under zipper Open side seams of other skirt. Pin triangles into side seams; sew. Try on; determine new hem length. Mark, turn, and sew hem.

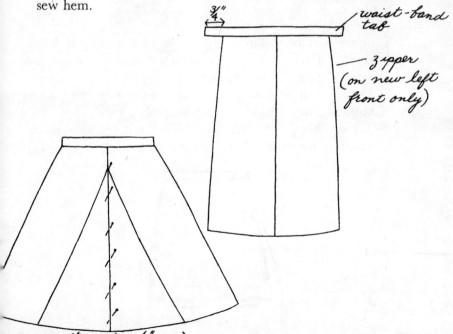

# Transformation #8:
# PANTSKIRT FROM AN OLD SKIRT

This is sportily smart to wear with Jamaica-or Bermuda-length shorts, and it is the easiest way I know to get extra mileage from an old pegged sheath skirt. I first did it for actress-model Suzy Parker, and now I do it all the time. It is so much more original than culottes, and great for long walks in town or country, for bicycling, for at home, patio parties, or just anywhere. Try matching a gray flannel to plaid shorts, or plum corduroy to yellow hopsacking. Or, of course, try whatever you've got on hand. You can even do it as an elegant evening outfit, working with a full-length narrow skirt and a pair of slacks.

*materials*

1 old skirt
3 to 4 yards ribbon lace
1 pair of Jamaica or Bermuda shorts, matching or contrasting
3 to 4 yards upholstery braid

*how-to*

1. Open skirt hem. Open side seams of skirt to just below zipper on left to the same point on the right. Attach ribbon lace to seam allowances and stitch down.
2. Pin braid up and down the four sides of skirt, and across bottom if desired. Sew.
3. Try on. Mark new hem length — make it the same as the length of the shorts. Turn and sew them.

4. Slip shorts into overskirt. Pin together through both waist-bands. If both have side zipper closings, tack together all around bottom of waistband. If one has back closing, tack together from left back to right side. (Or set snaps into both waistbands, using silk-covered ones to match the fabric of the shorts, so that the shorts can be worn without the overskirt as well.)


# Transformation #9:
# RE-EMBROIDERED SKIRT

This final skirt transformation is the answer if stains, cigarette burns, fading, tearing, or accidental damage of any kind have apparently ruined your favorite skirt. Wait! Don't discard it! Not until you've tried one of the following rescue ideas:

1. Embroider —chain stitches, daisies, or what-have-you (see Part VI) —all over the skirt. Cover the damaged portions thoroughly; then swirl your design freely to join the already-embroidered portions. This treatment is particularly effective on luxurious fabrics —brocades, velvets, silks —because you can get textural contrast by using a variety of threads and yarns. On brocade, let your stitches follow the design woven into the fabric. Long stems with leaves are always graceful to look at, and fairly quick and easy to stitch.
2. Appliqué —anything you like —over the damaged part. This will work best if the problem occurs near the hem, and/or in front. Use ready-made appliqués from your notions store; use a design cut out of a patterned fabric; cut your own design from a contrasting fabric. Stitch or paste down (see Part VI). If necessary, matching appliqués can be scattered over the skirt in several places, as needed or to form a new design.

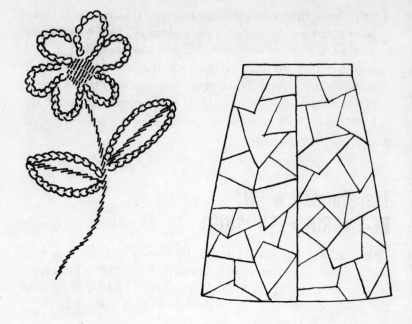

3. Sew beads, sequins, or paillettes over the damaged areas, and anywhere else over the skirt as well. Use beads to follow the woven pattern of a brocade, to outline the figures in a print, to highlight a floral-patterned fabric.

4. If a skirt has good lines, but is really worn and faded, use it as a foundation for patchwork. Follow directions below, Transformations #15 and #16, and in Part VI, for making patchwork garments. Use upholstery remnants, or anything in your ragbag, for patches, and crochet cord or embroidery thread. Remember that the patches must line up at the seams.

5. If the problem is merely fading, try drawing a scroll-like or vine design over the fabric with felt-tipped marking pens in suitable colors. This works wonders! (I've done it in dark pink on a lighter pink silk shirt, and it looks better now than it did when new.)

# Transformation #10:
# BATH SKIRT FROM A BATH TOWEL

Just the thing to wrap up in after the bath — and make a Bath Top to go with it. This is another version of Basic Style #4, the Jiffy Skirt. The border design of the bath towel is in the front of the skirt; a washcloth cuts a swathe as a pocket. And a king-size bath towel would make a cozy full-length skirt to wear in the evening — after your shower, or even, dressed up a bit with fringe, for entertaining.

*materials*

1 bath towel, at least 24″ wide (the width of the towel becomes the length of the skirt)
1 washcloth — matching or coordinated
1 yard ½″ elastic

*how-to*

1. Fold under 1½″ along one long side; stitch down to form casing for elastic.
2. Cut elastic to your waist measurement plus 1″. Use safety pin to pull through casing. Pin at both ends to secure.
3. Place two short ends together, wrong side out. Seam ½″ from edge, catching ends of elastic securely in stitching.
4. Try on. Determine best placing for pocket; mark with pins. Mark for hem if necessary; sew hem.
5. Sew on washcloth pocket.

6. Add any trimming that seems to belong (optional). Yarn fringe in matching or coordinated colors would be suitable; so would embroidered ribbon bands.

# Transformation #11:
# BATH TOP FROM TWO HAND TOWELS

This easy overblouse to complete your after-shower wardrobe requires only minutes of sewing.

*materials*
2 hand towels

*how-to*
1. Determine which way you will use the towels. If their width is at least 18″ (or half your bust measurement plus 2″), you can have the border at top and bottom, in a bateau neckline style that ends just on the shoulders (A). If their width is less, hold the towels the other way, with their borders forming a wide, short wing sleeve. (B).
2. Place towels with their right sides together. Fold down center and mark top center front and back with pin. Measure off 6″ on each side of pin and mark. Seam from these marks to ends.

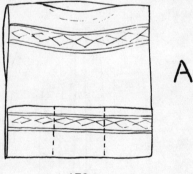

A

3. Try on. If head opening is too small, rip out ½″ of stitching on each side or more as necessary. Mark bottom of armhole where you like it—remember, this is an easy-fitting, *low* armhole. If overblouse seems too long for you, fold bottom *up* as necessary to form an apron-like pocket. Pin at bottom corners.
4. Sew side seams from bottom corners to pins marking underarm bottoms. If pocket treatment is being used, run rows of stitching up through pocket area as desired.
5. Trim around neckline, around bottom and/or around armhole (optional).

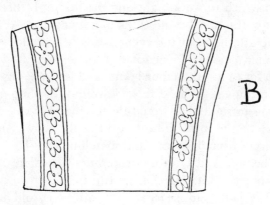

# Transformation #12:
# PARTY PANTS FROM PETTIPANTS

This is one of my newest creations, and if any invention was created by necessity, it is this evening-dress finishing touch for a dress-length outfit. One of my favorite customers came to me in a dither one day: she needed a luxurious gown to wear to a major film premiere—her husband was the producer— and she had to have it in less than a week. I knew I should have said it was impossible, but I decided I would do it. I designed an absolute dream of a gown, in yards and yards of creamy beige chiffon, gathered up in front with a brown velvet bow running from the high Empire bosom down to the floor-sweeping hem. To top it I designed a gracefully hooded brown velvet cloak, falling apart in front to reveal the lovely chiffon. I worked day and night on it, spending hours shopping for just the right fabric, stitching everything by hand. When my customer came for a fitting and told me that she had gotten me an invitation to the premiere too; that she would have a chauffeured limousine to pick me up; and that I would join her at the formal supper following the show, I was just too exhausted to give a thought to what I would wear. The big evening was only a few days off — I had only the weekend left in which to work night and day to finish the chiffon and velvet outfit, and I could think of nothing else. At four o'clock on the afternoon of the event I finally sent the gown to my customer, and as I collapsed I remembered — I was being called for in less than four hours, and for some reason I didn't have a thing to wear! I looked around the shop frantically — nothing in sight that would do for the designer of what was sure to be the most elegant outfit at the show. Ah, there was the lovely white lace tent and matching coat I had worn only once before. And I got my inspiration. I would take an extra piece of the white lace fabric, run up only two small seams, attach it quickly to the legs of my pettipants, and have evening trousers to wear under my dress. I am not being immodest when I report that my spur-of-the-moment outfit was a sensation.

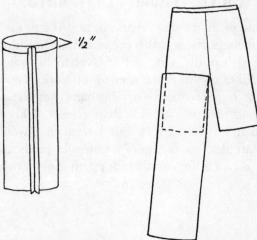

You too can make party pants, to go with or under practically anything. They would be particularly great under a tunic-length, Oriental-styled top, or with a mini-length dress. Wear them out for the most formal occasion, or at home to be a conversation-piece hostess. Make them, as I did, of lace; or make them of brocade, or velvet, or whatever you choose.

*materials*
1½ yards 36″ fabric
1 pair pettipants

*how-to*
1. Cut fabric so that you have two pieces about 24″ wide and 36″ long. Each will be one leg.
2. Turn under ½″ at top of each piece; stitch. Place both long sides of fabric together, with right sides facing, and seam ½″ from edge to form tubes.
3. Turn right sides out. Place pettipants inside so that seams of tubes are on inside and turned-under edge at top of pettipants leg. Stitch tubes to pettipants just at crotch.
4. Try on; mark desired length for hem. Sew hem.

# Transformation #13:
## LITTLE BAG TO MATCH ANYTHING FROM AN OLD OR INEXPENSIVE BAG

Ever wish for a handbag to match a special outfit? Who hasn't! Now you can make it yourself, using whatever fabric you want. All you need is a fabric bag of the size and shape you choose. Use a worn-out clutch that may be hiding in a corner of your closet, or buy an inexpensive one in any dime store. You can also make a new lining for any bag.

*materials*

1 fabric-covered hand bag—the kind with a metal clasp frame at the top
½ yard (approximately) any fabric for outside of bag
½ yard (approximately) any fabric for lining (optional)
½ yard velvet ribbon or lace

*how-to*

1. First make lining if desired. Place bag on wrong side of folded fabric and draw outline. Add ½″ all around for seam allowance. Cut in two. Place together with right sides facing and make ½″ seam around sides and bottom. Place inside bag. Turn top under ½″ and stitch down just below frame. Do not worry about making stitches invisible either inside or outside the bag. The stitches on the inside will later be covered with ribbon or lace; the stitches that go through to the outside will be hidden by the new bag covering. (*Note:* Of course, if you are only adding a new lining to a bag that is otherwise in good condition, take care not to have lining stitches going completely through to outside of bag.)
2. Trace outline of bag on wrong side of folded outer fabric. Add ½″ all around for seam allowance; cut two. Sew

176

½″ seam at bottom. Place over bag, being sure bottom seams of covering and of bag meet. Turn sides and top under ½″ all around, pinning in place at side bag seams and just below frame. Stitch carefully, making sure stitches do not show on top; but don't worry about their coming through to lining side.

3. Cut ribbon or lace long enough to cover inside edges just below frame; sew lightly in place to hide stitching. Make a tack right through all layers of lining and outside of bag at bottom seam center, as shown; this will hold the bag firmly in place.

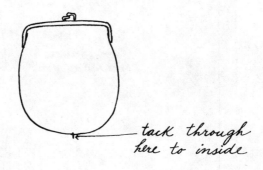

*tack through here to inside*

# Transformation #14:
# BABY'S SOAKERS

Here's a useful gift for the youngest in the family. Dress-up waterproof panties to peek out fron under the teeniest skirts or shirts—for baby boys as well as baby girls these soakers are an essential item of wearing apparel. You can make them to match or go with anything, or just make them whimsically attractive, as in a miniature blue jean with a patch pocket in back. Just make sure all trimmings are washable.

*materials*

1 pair waterproof plastic baby pants, snap-on style
½ yard fabric
ribbon, strips of fabric, lace, etc., for trim as desired

*how-to*

1. Use plastic pants as a pattern, stretching them out where
   they are elasticized at back of waist and inside leg. Trace
   full outline on heavy paper. Add on extra ½″ seam allowance all around. Pin to fabric; cut out.

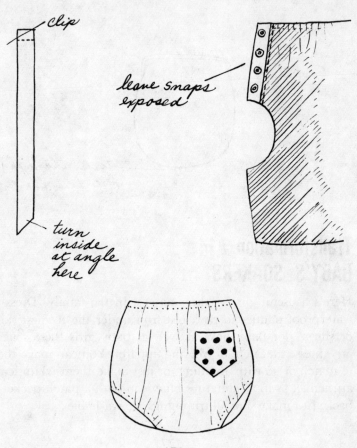

clip

leave snaps
exposed

turn
inside
at angle
here

2. Turn in ½″ all around; pin to plastic pants, making sure pins go through edges of plastic pants only. Stitch down, using back stitch or combination stitch, *very close to edge*. At sides where pants snap, fold in enough extra fabric and stitch down on seam line, leaving snaps exposed.
3. Add on trimmings as desired. See sketches for suggestions. For large bow, cut two strips of fabric 18″ by 3″. Fold in half lengthwise, wrong side out; seam ½″ from edge; turn, shape as shown, press, and sew into side of back of pants.

# Transformation #15:
# MAN'S AT-HOME VEST

I make these elegant evening vests to order in my shop, and charge a minimum of $200 for them; you can make one for your favorite man for the tiniest fraction of that amount. Use a vest that he has discarded as the foundation for patchwork and embroidery; find luxurious remnants of upholstery fabric—brocades, cut velvets, jacquard weaves—and use also bits and pieces cut from his old neckties—foulards, paisleys. Three vests—of gold antique cut velvet, of velvet-embroidered needlepoint in muted shades, and of an Oriental-patterned fabric—that I made for Dr. Joseph Santo, the New York dentist who created and owns those very "in" restaurants, Sign of the Dove and Yellowfinger, were shown in *Gentlemen's Quarterly*, which advised wearing them with white or pastel shirts and solid color neckties.

*materials*
1 man's vest (any fabric will do)
scraps of brocade, cut velvet, other fabrics
buttons (see below)
embroidery floss

*how-to*
1. Remove buttons from vest. Carefully open side and bottom lining seams so you can work easily through vest, leaving lining attached at top and front. Cut fabric into pieces to make patchwork. Sew and embroider according to instructions in Part VI. In sewing patchwork to vest, remember that all seam and dart lines on the vest must be repeated in the patchwork. Sew patches onto vest. Leave ½" of patches hanging over all seam lines, dart lines, and outer edges of vest. When entire vest has been covered with patchwork, turn the ½" overhang inside (that is, to wrong side of patchwork, on top of old vest, and pin down. Stitch invisibly. Embroider over patch joinings and inside patches.
2. If you like, make welt pocket flaps out of solid color, perhaps black or tan, velvet; do not embroider. Leave back of vest as it is. Sew lining back in place.
3. You can use the old buttons, but it is nicer to get suitably luxurious new ones—pearl or gold, perhaps. You can make new buttonholes through patchwork exactly over the old ones, and sew the buttons in place. Or you can attach silk-covered snaps as a closing, and sew buttons in place over them on outside of vest.

180

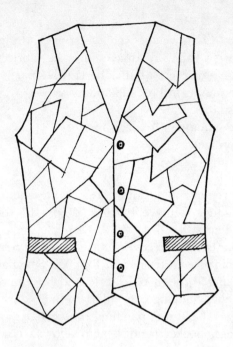

# Transformation #16:
# THEATER COAT

The same trick that transformed an ordinary vest into something extra special will provide you with a theater or evening coat that will be the envy of everyone. I make these to order for several hundred dollars — you can make one yourself for as little as $10 or $20! Start with an old coat with very good lines (even a bathrobe might do as a foundation); cover it with velvet and/or brocade patches, lushly embroidered; make a new lining from pale silk or striped taffeta.

*materials*

1 fabric coat (a lightweight wool, such as a spring or trans-
season coat; a raincoat — make sure the fabric is easy to
sew through — or even a bathrobe that is smartly styled)
upholstery remnants in brocade and/or velvet
silk-covered snaps
3 yards (approximately) lining fabric
6 yards ribbon lace

*how-to*

1. Carefully remove old lining; reserve to use as pattern
   for new lining. Remove buttons, snaps, any other trim.
   Let down hem.
2. Cut remnants into pieces to make patches. Sew together
   and embroider as instructed in Part VI. Sew patches onto
   coat, working through old fabric and interlinings. Leave
   ½″ of patches hanging over all seam lines, dart lines, and
   pocket edges. Continue patching onto collar, pocket flaps,
   front facings, pocket facings, hem allowance, sleeve-hem
   allowances—everywhere original fabric appears. When
   one area of coat, such as the right front, is completely
   covered with patchwork, turn ½″ seam allowance under
   and pin in place along seam lines. Sew down. Then continue patching over next area of coat. When entire coat
   is covered with fabric patches, begin embroidering.
   Embroider over joined edges, and also inside individual
   fabric patches. See suggested embroidery stitches in
   Part VI.
3. Use old lining as pattern for cutting new one. Be sure
   to leave ½″ seam allowance all around, and 2″ hem
   allowance at bottom. Sew new lining together—side
   seams, shoulder seams, sleeve seams, insert sleeves—in
   sequence. Insert lining into coat as the old one had been.
   See "linings," Part VI.

182

4. Turn up hem to desired length; pin and sew. Turn up lining hem about 2″ higher than coat hem; pin and sew. Join lining to coat body near hemline at side seams only, by attaching a 2″ length of crocheted heavy duty sewing thread through seams.
5. Pin ribbon lace all around inside of coat, over lining where it joins patchwork facing. Sew down.
6. Sew silk-covered snaps in place, starting at neckline and placing them every 3″. Use four, five, or more snaps as desired.
7. If desired, narrow round upholstery braid in black, gold, or other color can be used to outline any or all of these: collar, front edges, hem, sleeve bottom, pocket opening, hem bottom.

# Transformation #17:
# SUNNY DAY COAT

If I have any favorites among my many creations, this is surely one of them. I start with an old poplin raincoat—worn and perhaps torn, certainly stained and no longer water repellent. After decorating it all over —so easily, with pasted-on appliqués and painted-on designs—I add a new terry-cloth lining. A thorough spraying with a can of water-repellent protects the coat and returns it to service. When I travel, this is usually the only coat I take along —to wear day and evening, for, train, plane and theater, and even as a bathrobe or dressing gown!

Don't wait —just look in *your* closet to find the basic ingredient for your Sunny Day Coat.

*materials*

1 worn poplin raincoat

3 yards fabric (approximately) for lining (terry cloth, denim, corduroy, fake fur, mattress ticking are suitable)

1 yard cotton fabric printed with a design suitable for cutting out (fruits, flowers, animals, paper dolls, toy soldiers, autumn leaves, butterflies, vegetables) — chintz usually has good printed designs

embroidery floss

fabric glue

felt-tipped marking pens in one or several colors

1 aerosol spray can water-repellent

new buttons

*how-to*

1. Remove buttons from raincoat; remove any trim. Carefully remove lining and reserve.
2. Cut designs out of patterned cotton cloth. It is not necessary to leave a margin of fabric to be turned under, as in standard appliqué; cut the designs out as though you were cutting paper. Place on coat to cover stains, worn spots, and wherever you like. Pin in place so you can see the new pattern of your coat emerging. When you are satisfied with the arrangement, glue the designs down, using just a spot of glue on the raincoat under the design; wait until it gets slightly tacky—about a minute—and press the design firmly in place. When most or all of the designs have been glued down, start working an overcast stitch around the edges of the designs.
3. Connect the designs with scrolls, leaves, and vines, or other patterns drawn on with felt-tipped marking pens. (My Sunny Day Coat has green stems and leaves intertwined with a fruit-and-vegetable print; watermelons of pink are overcast with green embroidery floss; golden bananas with brown; and so on.)

185

4. Use the old lining as a pattern for the new, allowing ½″ seam allowance all around, and a 2″ hem allowance. Sew new lining together—side seams, shoulder seams, sleeve seams, insert sleeves—in sequence. Insert new lining into coat as the old one had been.
5. Adjust hem of coat, if necessary. Turn up lining hem about 2″ higher than coat hem; pin and sew.
6. Sew on new buttons.

# Transformation #18:
# DENIM DRESS-UPS

Here is more magic to work with appliqués, a few odds and ends, and lots of imagination. Dungarees, work shirts, overalls—anything in blue denim—takes beautifully to the brightening effect of colorful cotton appliqué. Beads, sequins, and dime-store "jewels" will help give you the kookiest coveralls in town. I have given this treatment to red-denim items for children—a little vest had a spread of cards poking out of its pocket, a snowman cavorted on a tiny diaper cover, and butterflies and flowers scattered across petite dungarees. For Celeste Holm I adorned a blue coverall with such whimsies as a pair of pert kittens and a green leaf tied with a red velvet bow and glittering with red sequins. An Army-Navy surplus store is good source of supply of garments to decorate.

*materials*

dungarees or other garment of blue or red denim (or any other
   solid-color durable fabric — chino, for example)
scraps of printed cotton fabric with designs to be cut out
fabric glue
embroidery floss
sequins, beads, fake "jewels" (optional)

1. Cut out designs from cotton fabric. Place them on denim garment. If garment is old, place appliqués to conceal worn spots. Pin in place until you have your arrangement worked out.
2. Use fabric glue to secure appliqués to garment. Apply glue to garment, wait a minute until it is slightly tacky, and press appliqué in place.
3. When glue is dry, embroider around edges of appliqués. Work embroidered stems and leaves, for flowers, embroidered feelers for butterflies. Sew or glue beads or sequins for eyes of animals or figures, for centers of flowers. If you have appliquéd a hand, give it a jeweled ring or bracelet. Sequins or jet beads can be the hours on a clock face, the tie clasp on a necktie, the collar on a poodle, the buttons on a clown. . . . You take it from there!

## Transformations #19-24

From now on, really, you're on your own. I will just give you a half dozen ideas and sketches of other transformations I have wrought. Using these ideas, and the techniques depended upon in the above, more detailed instructions, I'm sure you can go on to redesign almost anything you come across.

café curtains as a short, short 20's cocktail dress

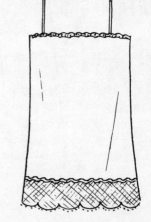

188

*pinch-pleated curtain becomes — an empire-waisted skirt*

# Transformation #19:
# CURTAIN SKIRT

I have made a wonderful, Empire-waisted skirt out of a half of a pair of ready-made curtains. The pinch pleating becomes the high cinched-in waist; a back zipper or hook-and-eye closing gets you in and out; and all you have to do is adjust the hem. If it is weighted, so much the better: it will hang just beautifully on you. Use a longer curtain for an evening skirt, a café curtain for a short-short one.

# Transformation #20:
## SHOES OR SNEAKERS TO MATCH ANYTHING

You can make sneakers to match your denim dress-ups or anything else (Transformation #18 above); or you can have a pair of fabric shoes to match any outfit. Fabric glue is your secret. Use it to press small appliqués onto sneakers; or to attach patches of any fabric (scraps left from dressmaking, or from shortening a hem) to a fabric shoe. Just overlap round and triangular patches, no bigger than 2″ across, all over your shoes. Be sure to have straight edges of the patches meet at the rear seam line of your shoe. I did this with scraps of white lace to match the outfit described in Transformation #12. The fabric patches will mold to the shape of the shoe when they are spread with glue; when dry they will stick forever. Finish off with a water-repellent treatment from a spray can, and you won't have to worry about sudden showers. Note: sneakers can be quickly colored to match anything by using a felt-tipped marking pen; or they can be tinted with a sponge dipped in a cup of dye.

# Transformation #21:
## LUNCHBOX HANDBAG

Would you believe that an ordinary lunch box, such as all schoolchildren carry, makes a most unusual handbag? I bought a pink one with a white poodle waiting for a school bus on it, and by pasting on braid and dime-store "jewels" dressed it up so it could go out on the town with a most elegant matron. Paste a cloth lining inside, with lace or trim pasted over its edges. Paste braid on the metal handle; or paint it gold. Paint the latch gold.

# Transformation #22:
## DISCOTHEQUE DRESS

My too-long leopard-printed nylon petticoat has just become the shortest of discotheque dresses. The waistband, of course, is the new low, low neckline, so low it goes under the arms as well. Narrow black braid covers the neckline edges, and forms the straps that hold it up. Rows of braid also top the narrow black lace hem, and add just enough weight to this packable dancing dress to make it really swing.

# Transformation #23:
# PIGTAIL HAT

Take one inexpensive straw hat, add a big fat hatband of yarn, and continue the yarn in two big braids hanging well down from the brim. Tie them with big, bright schoolgirl bows.

# Transformations #24:
# MANY-POCKETED APRONS

A fabric shoebag makes three aprons, with pockets to hold sewing equipment, gardening supplies, or home handyman's tools. Just cut across between each row of pockets, add a wide, bright velvet ribbon as a waistband and sash, and decorate the pockets with pasted-on appliqués to your heart's content. Narrow velvet ribbon can be used to bind the edges.

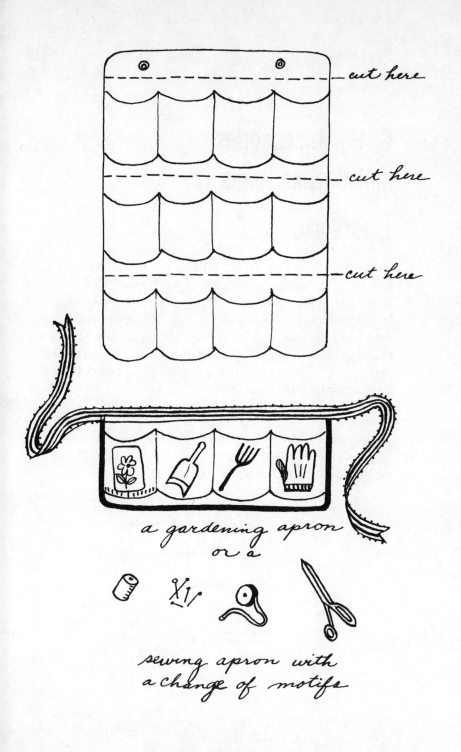

cut here

cut here

cut here

a gardening apron
or a

sewing apron with
a change of motifs

# V

# Gifts, Accessories and Bazaar Items

## 1. TOTE BAG

Make this up in any size, any fabric; it will go anywhere, at any hour of the day or evening. I have done luxurious totes in antique patchwork and leather, and work-a-day ones in a bandanna-print cotton lined and trimmed with heavy denim. I'll use this version for our example; but first let me suggest that you try it in a gay printed vinyl-coated fabric, perhaps lined with corduroy; or in a combination of upholstery remnants, perhaps a heavy brocade lined with velour.

*materials*

1 piece each bandanna print and heavy denim, each piece
   measuring 18″ x 44″; and two strips of denim 2½″ x 16″
eyelets and tools for attaching (optional)

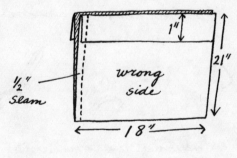

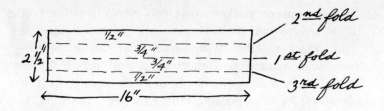

*how-to*

1. Fold bandanna print in half crosswise with right sides together. Fold down 1″ across top and pin. Sew side seams ½″ from edge. Turn right side out.
2. Repeat with denim.
3. Make two straps of denim; fold long strips to inside lengthwise three times as shown and topstitch ⅛″ from folded edges.

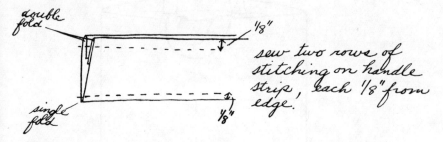

*sew two rows of stitching on handle strip, each ⅛″ from edge.*

4. Fasten straps to wrong side of denim bag as shown: stitch firmly as in sketch, or use eyelets.
5. Place denim bag inside bandanna-print bag, wrong sides together. Join by sewing (either topstitch or hand stitch) *around top only.*

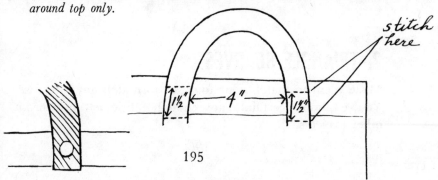

*stitch here*

6. To make outside pockets: take two pieces of either fabric 10″ x 18″, or one piece denim and one piece bandanna print. Place together with rights sides facing. Sew ½″ from edge around two short sides and one long side. Turn; pin in place in center of one side of bag, with raw edges at bottom of pocket. Turn raw edges to inside; pin and stitch. Stitch up center of pocket to make two pockets. Stitch sides of pockets to side seams of bag.

*Note:* If your choice of fabrics does not provide enough firmness, cut a piece of interfacing 18″ x 42″. Place it between the folds on one piece of fabric in step 1.

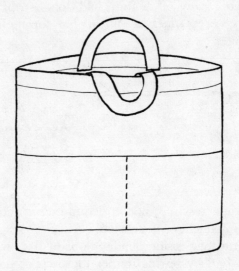

## 2. TRIANGLE SCARVES

Make them to match your totes, or to match anything else. You've almost certainly got enough fabric left over from other projects.

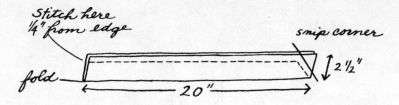

Stitch here ¼" from edge

snip corner

fold

2½"

20"

*materials*

2 triangles of fabric, 11" x 11" x 15½" (either matching or contrasting)

2 long strips of fabric 2½" x 20"

*how-to*

1. Make ties first: fold long strips in half lengthwise, right sides facing. Sew across one end at an angle and along the long edge ¼" from edge, as shown. Clip angled end. Turn right side out, using blunt end of pencil or knitting needle to push material through. Repeat with second strip.
2. Place triangles together with right sides facing. Sew around ½" from edge, leaving three openings as shown. Cut off corners. Turn right side out through opening in long side. Hand sew to close up opening.
3. Place open end of each tie in one of the side openings. Stitch close to edge to hold ties in place.

*Note:* It's just as easy to make a triangle for a little girl. The long side of the triangle is about 12", the short sides 8½", and the ties about 12".

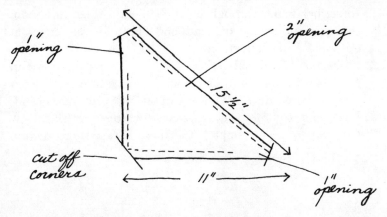

opening 1"

2" opening

15½"

cut off corners

11"

1" opening

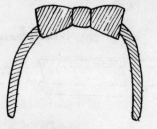

# 3. HEADBANDS

Make these by the dozen, from leftover pieces of fabric; you can match any skirt or dress. If you use woolens or velvets the headbands will grip your hair firmly and stay in place securely.

*materials*

1 plastic headband, about ½″ wide

a strip of fabric as long as the length of the headband plus ¾″, and as wide as two times the width of the headband plus ¾″ (if headband is 11½″ long and ½″ wide, strip of fabric should be 12¼″ long by 1¾″ wide)

strip of fabric 2½″ x 10″ or 1½″ x 7″ (optional) for sew-on bow or tie-on knot

*how-to*

1. Fold strip of fabric in half lengthwise with right sides together and stitch around one short end and long unfolded edge ¼″ from edge. Turn right side out, using blunt end of pencil or knitting needle.

2. Insert headband through unstitched end. Make sure seam comes on underside of headband. Turn in raw edges at open end and stitch closed.

3. Make bow (optional): Fold 2½″ x 10″ strip of fabric in half lengthwise, right sides facing; make seam ¼″ from edge on long side only. Turn. Cut off 2½″ piece at one end. Fold long section twice so that raw edges overlap; sew (or glue or even staple) together. Wrap short section

around middle of bow so that its raw edges meet; sew (or glue) raw edges together. Sew or glue bow onto headband.

4. Or make optional tie-on knot: Fold 1½" x 7" strip of fabric in half lengthwise with right sides facing; sew seam ¼" from edge on long side only. Turn, using blunt end of pencil or knitting needle to push through. Tie around center of headband. Turn raw edges of short ends to inside.

## 4. FLOWER PETAL HAT

A wonderful remnant of bright cotton with flowers of several sizes and colors was the inspiration for this hat. You can duplicate it with any similarly patterned fabric; or you can make your own cut-out flowers from whatever scraps of material you have on hand.

This hat uses a nylon curler cap as a base; but it can be as smart and dressy as you like. You can also build it over an old pillbox or toque or any other hat shape you have on hand or can pick up inexpensively—whatever style looks well on you.

*materials*

½ yard fabric printed with large flowers or pieces of fabric
   from which you cut your own flowers
felt-tipped marking pens in various colors (if you will cut your
   own flowers)
extra-strong fabric glue
nylon or cotton curler cap, or other hat base
circle, about 6″ in diameter, of interfacing (optional—if hat
   base used has not enough body to suit you)
button, pompon, or ball taken from ball fringe
clear varnish aerosol spray

*how-to*

1. Cut out flowers from fabric. You will need 7 to 10 flowers:

   2 or 3 flowers, about 3″ diameter,
   1 or 2 flowers, about 5″ diameter,
   1 or 2 flowers, about 7″ diameter,
   and 1 flower each: about 9″ and/or 11″, and 13″ or 14″
   diameter (Dimensions are approximate; please, do not
   worry if the flowers in your pattern are 2½″ or 6″ across;
   use what you have. You might be able to combine two or
   three smaller ones to get the effect of a larger one.)
2. *Or* make your own flowers. Use these sketches as ideas,
   and draw flowers on different colored fabric scraps with
   felt-tipped marking pens — black, green, or whatever colors
   you like.
3. If hat base you are using does not have sufficient body,
   paste and/or sew circle of interfacing to top of crown.
   Attach at center and around sides.
4. Begin arranging flowers: start by placing largest flower
   at top center of hat so that its petals droop gracefully
   down to cover bottom. If necessary, cut more deeply
   into petals, slashing almost to the center, so that they
   fall more freely. When flower is arranged the way you
   like it, glue it in the center and at petal ends so they stay

200

in place around hat edge. Place next largest flower in center, arrange its petals, and glue in place. Continue, alternating colors attractively, until all but the smallest flowers are used. End, perhaps, by gluing two small flowers slightly off center. There should be five or six layers of flowers.

5. Sew or glue button, pompon, or ball from ball fringe in center. Glue down petals of flowers where necessary.
6. Spray lightly with a coat of clear varnish.

# 5. THREE EARRINGS

These are simply made, using earring backs you can buy in the five-and-ten or any hobby or notions store. Make them to match any outfit, by covering large domed button shapes with fabric. Or make them whimsical, like a cluster of small shining safety pins tied with a teeny velvet bow. Or make them . . .

a.　　　　　　　b.　　　　　　　c.

*a. Tweed Earrings*

Select a pair of rounded wooden or plastic buttons, without shanks, in the size most becoming to you. Cut two fabric circles, about twice the diameter of the button. Put some strong white glue on the wrong side of the fabric circle, place a button face down on it and press fabric all around button with fingers, stretching and smoothing fabric until button is completely covered and raw edges of fabric meet at bottom of button. A drop or two of glue will secure raw edges. Glue to earring backs. Use fabric scraps left over from your sewing: tweed, to match a coat or suit; velvet; or anything else you have on hand.

*b. Safety Pin Earrings*

Buy a bunch or a card of the small-size safety pins—1″ is fine—in gold, chrome, or black. Gather up eight or ten of them on narrow velvet ribbon, and tie a tiny bow. Glue to earring back. Repeat for second earring.

*c. Gilded Nut Earrings*

Gild two walnut-shell halves by painting or spraying with gold paint or enamel. Make two loops of velvet ribbon in the color of your choice from two strips about 1″ x 3″; glue ends of ribbon onto walnut-shell backs. (Or glue ribbon into shells first; then spray gold to gild ribbon and shells.) Glue or sew tops of ribbon loops to earring backs. (For dangling earrings, use 5″ lengths of ribbon.)

# 6. AND TWO NECKLACES

Make these to go with everything, too. To match your Tweed Earrings, how about a string of Tweed Beads? And just a few real gilt or glittery beads combine with bright silk cords and yarns to swing long and gaily around or loop over and over around your neck.

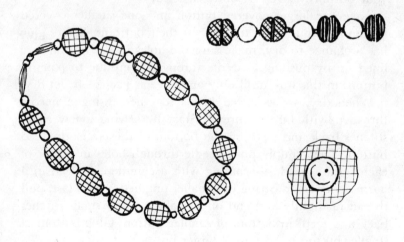

*a. Tweed Beads*

To make an opera-length necklace, you need 54 rounded wooden or plastic buttons about ¾″ in diameter; 54 of the same type button one size smaller, about ½″ in diameter; and

54 commercial beads (from an old necklace, a dime-store necklace, or a package), about ¼" in diameter. The buttons should not have shanks, but should have holes going right through. You also need scraps of tweed or other fabric, strong white glue, and a spool of extra-strong button thread.

Cut a piece of fabric into one circle about 1½" in diameter and another circle 1" in diameter. Put some glue on the wrong side of the larger fabric circle and press the top of a larger button down on it. Bring edges of fabric up all around and work with fingers until button is completely covered with fabric. Raw edges of fabric should come together on bottom of button. Add a drop or two of glue to hold them secure and flat. Repeat with smaller fabric circle and a smaller button. If fabric circles are the right size to fit smoothly around buttons, cut 53 more circles in each size and continue to cover buttons with fabric. If not, experiment with slightly larger or slightly smaller fabric circles until you find the size that fits your buttons. Cover all buttons; let dry.

Take one larger covered button and one smaller covered button and glue them together at their bottoms. Before glue has a chance to dry, make sure the holes in the buttons are lined up by pushing a needle through. Continue to pair off buttons in this way until only one of each size is left; let dry.

When dry, string tweed beads together, using a needle threaded with button thread. Start by sewing a few small stitches back and forth on the bottom of the larger unglued button. Then simply push needle through holes in center of each button bead, alternating with a commercial bead in a harmonious color. String the smaller unglued button last; pull thread up tightly and end off by taking a few small stitches back and forth in bottom of smaller button. Glue bottom of smaller button to bottom of larger button; let dry.

Larger or smaller necklaces may be made by using more or fewer beads. For a smaller necklace, it will be necessary to sew the end beads into a necklace clasp.

Buttons can be covered in the same or in several different fabrics; I like to make them to match a skirt or coat.

## b. Twisted Thread Necklace

Use any interesting or attractive heavy thread or decorative cord — crochet cord, embroidery floss, chenille, silk-wool yarn, gold-wrapped or beaded thread. Combine several different colors and textures. If your threads are thin, as embroidery floss, combine six or eight; if as thick as package cord, you might use two or three combined with two or three strands of a thinner, contrasting thread. Determine the length you want your necklace to be; double it and add 5". Cut all your threads this length. For instance, if you want a short, choker-length necklace of about 17", cut your threads 39" long. Knot them together at top. Attach to a cup hook or door knob for easy working. Twist, twist, and twist the threads until they are quite tightly twisted. Then, holding the loose ends firmly at the bottom with one hand, run the other hand down the twisted part to keep it from tangling. Bring the hand holding the loose end up to the knot at the top, letting the twisted cords twist up again on itself. Knot tightly again at the top to hold firmly. Cut off excess thread close to knot. Attach both ends — the knotted one and the folded one — to a clasp such as the one illustrated by sewing firmly. (If desired, instead of cutting off extra threads at knotted end, leave them dangling in 3" lengths. Thread a gold or other bead onto one, two, or three thread ends, and make a small tight knot to hold the bead in place.)

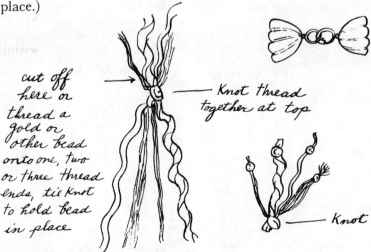

cut off here or thread a gold or other bead onto one, two or three thread ends, tie knot to hold bead in place

— Knot thread together at top

— Knot

# 7. TAPE MEASURE BELT

From a standard 60″ tape measure you can make a clever, original belt.

*materials*

1 tape measure, fabric or plastic (these come in several colors)
2 yards ⅞″ grosgrain ribbon or ¼ yard felt
3 silk-covered snaps
two small (travel-kit size) spools of sewing thread
strong fabric glue

*how-to*

1. Cut 60″ length of grosgrain ribbon; *or* cut strip of felt 60″ long and ⅞″ wide. Use fabric glue to attach felt backing to tape measure.
2. Fit tape measure around your waist. Make a half knot, letting the ends drop to the length you want. Mark placing of three snaps under knot to hold ends in place. Sew on snaps.
3. Attach one spool of thread to each end of belt, sewing through tape measure and felt. (There usually is a hole in the metal staple at the end of the tape measure; sew through this hole.) If desired, a small pair of sewing scissors can be tied to one end of belt with a narrow piece of ribbon; a small pincushion can also be tied on.

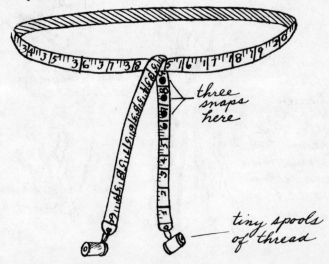

three snaps here

tiny spools of thread

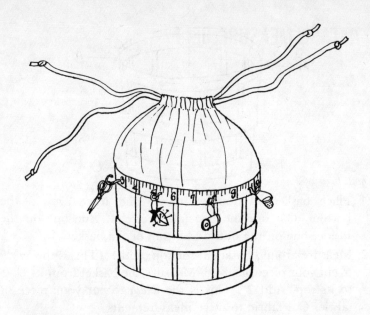

# 8. SEWING BASKET

Take a peach basket, top it with fabric, and close it with a drawstring. Hang scissors, pincushion, and spools of thread from cup hooks around the outside. And you have a pretty, practical sewing basket in which to tote your needlework from room to room, or to give as a gift or to sell for a tidy profit at a bazaar.

*materials*

1 peach basket, any size you like
½ to 1 yard any fabric (the larger the peach basket, the more fabric you will need)
1 to 2 yards yarn, cord, or tubing for drawstring
1 tape measure
6 to 12 cup hooks; several small screw eyes
sewing notions, such as spools of thread, small sewing scissors, pin cushion
strong fabric glue

207

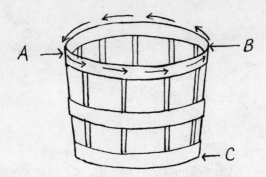

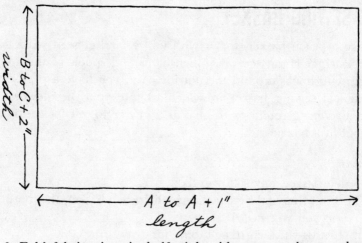

*how-to*

1. Place basket on doubled fabric and trace around the bottom. Cut out the two fabric circles; glue one on the inside, one on the outside bottom of the basket.

2. Measure around basket at the top; add 1″. This is the *length* to cut your piece of fabric. Measure the basket from its base to its top. Add 2″. This is the *width* to cut your piece of fabric. Cut fabric to these measurements.

3. Fold fabric piece in half, right sides out, and seam short ends together ½″ from edge, forming a tube that will fit around rim of basket. At top of tube fold down ¼″ to wrong side; then fold down 1″ to wrong side. Stitch at bottom of 1″ fold to form casing for drawstring.

4. Turn tube right side out. Make two cuts at opposite sides of casing, slashing from fold at top almost to stitching. Work small blanket or buttonhole stitch around cut edges.
5. Cut yarn or cord for drawstring in half. Use a safety pin to pull one strand through one opening in casing, around through casing so that both ends of strand come out through same opening. Repeat with second strand and second casing opening. See sketch. Knot ends of drawstring.
6. Glue bottom edge of tube to inside rim of basket.
7. Glue tape measure around outer rim of basket. Cut off excess. Screw cup hooks through tape measure into rim. Attach small screw eyes to the wooden tops of several spools of thread in basic colors—certainly black and white, perhaps brown, blue, yellow, red. Hang spools on cup hooks. Attach a small loop of yarn or cord to a sewing scissors and a pin cushion; hang on other cup hooks.

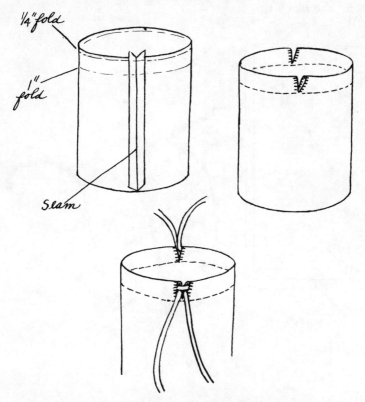

# 9. THREE BIBS

I make these out of washable felt; but they might be more practical done in vinyl.

*a. Ladybug Bib*

You need a 12″ x 12″ square of red felt and a 12″ x 12″ square of cotton knit or flannelette (a receiving blanket or a layette kimono would do) *or* a 12″ x 12″ square of red vinyl (vinyls are bonded to cotton-knit backings); scraps of yellow and black felt or vinyl; and 1 yard black rickrack. Cut out the bib according to the sketch, cutting one each from red felt and cotton knit *or* one from red vinyl. Use fabric glue to paste rickrack down center and at corners as shown; to paste on spots made of ½″ pieces of rickrack; to paste on black felt or vinyl tip of ladybug; and to paste two yellow felt or vinyl eyes on the black tip.

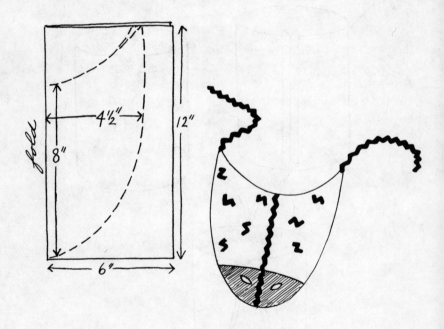

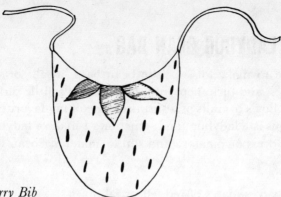

*b. Strawberry Bib*

The strawberry bib requires the same amount of red felt and cotton knit *or* vinyl as the ladybug bib, and is cut to the same basic shape. Use green bias binding for ties, and either glue or sew on. Cut three leaves from green felt or vinyl and glue at top of "strawberry." Use black felt-tipped marking pen to make the spots.

*c. Clown Bib*

Your own imagination can take over on this one. Use any color felt or vinyl that you like; 12″ squares are again cut to the same basic shape. Any ribbon or bias binding can make the ties. Scraps of white felt provide circles for the eyes and a large oval for the mouth; glue on. Other felt scraps could be glued on for ears, nose, cheeks. Or features can be "painted" on with felt-tipped markers: hair, crosses in center of white circles for eyes, smaller red oval inside large white one for mouth.

*Note:* If you work with vinyl, staystitch around cut out main piece before adding pasted or sewn decorations.

# 10. LADYBUG BEAN BAG

I like to make lots of little bean bags, in all sorts of funny shapes, and tuck them into the pocket of a little girl's dress or little boy's overalls as a surprise. One of my favorite bean-bag designs is a ladybug; and sometimes I make a ladybug pocket on a dress or pinafore and slip its matching bean bag inside.

*materials*

2 5″ x 5″ squares of red felt or fabric
2 3″ x 3″ squares of black felt (or a 4″ strip of black velvet ribbon, 2″ wide)
yellow felt scraps *or* 2 small yellow buttons
pea beans
felt-tipped marking pen, black

*how-to*

1. Cut two egg-shaped pieces from the red felt, as shown. Cut two black half-ovals as shown.
2. Seam or glue each black piece to one of the red pieces as shown.
3. Sew button eyes or glue felt eyes in place on black part of one piece. Glue black felt scrap dots or use black felt-tipped marking pen to make spots and stripe as shown.
4. Place both pieces together with their wrong sides facing and topstitch around very close to edge, leaving a 2″ opening at top.
5. Stuff bean bag with pea beans through opening. Hand sew closed.

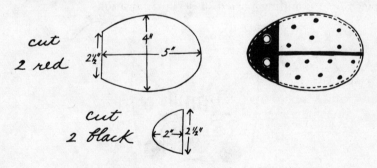

cut
2 red
4″
5″
2½″

cut
2 black
2″
2½″

# 11. CORD-HOLDER APPLE

The cuff of a worn red sweater, or a red replacement knit cuff that you can buy at a notions counter, makes a wonderful bazaar or house gift that is practical, too.

*materials*
1 red knit cuff (3″ to 4″ long)
scraps of green felt
ball of household cord or twine

*how-to*
1. Gather top of cuff to close. If it had a raw edge, first sew a narrow piece of ribbon or seam binding to edge to prevent raveling. Cut leaves out of green felt; glue or sew to top of "apple," concealing stitches.
2. Put ball of twine inside apple, with end of twine hanging down through bottom opening. Gather edge of cuff at bottom opening, pulling around twine only tightly enough so that twine can be pulled through.

*Note:* A larger ball of twine could be concealed in a purple or dark blue knit cuff, made to look like an eggplant. Or a green cuff could be a green apple.

213

# 12. HOT PLATE

You can make a hot plate to go with any kitchen or dining room decor, at a cost of absolutely nothing! Simply use scraps of fabric — left over from your kitchen curtains, or perhaps from some stained and worn tablecloth or napkins — and sew them around soda-bottle caps. What could be easier? And it's a welcome gift, too.

*materials*
scraps of fabric
28 or more soda-bottle caps

*how-to*
1. Using one bottle cap as a pattern, draw around it on cardboard. Enlarge the resulting circle by ½″ all around, forming a pattern circle that is 1″ larger in diameter than the bottle cap.
2. Use the pattern circle to mark and cut out 28 fabric circles.
3. Hand sew small running stitches around one fabric circle ⅛″ from edge. Place a bottle cap inside the fabric circle and pull thread to gather running stitches tightly. Fasten thread securely. Repeat until all bottle caps have been covered with fabric circles.
4. Working from the wrong side, stitch the discs together as shown to form hot plate. (It can also be made in diamond or circle shape.)

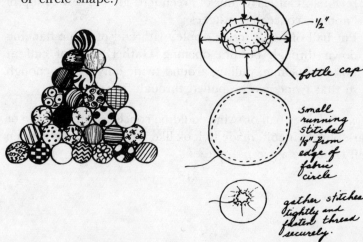

# 13. PIGGY BANK (OR DOGGY BANK)

An empty white plastic bleach bottle, some felt or other fabric, and the odds and ends everyone has around the house, make a whimsical piggy bank.

*materials*

an empty white plastic bleach bottle (the smallest size is a little pig, or perhaps a dachshund or basset hound for a doggy bank; the large bottles are big, fat pigs)

felt — perhaps pink for the pig, tan for the dachshund — a large enough piece to wrap the plastic bottle

*or* any other fabric — possibly an upholstery remnant

*or* yarn

*or* a can of gold (or any other color) spray paint

a 6″ length of twine, yarn, wire, string; or a silk tassel or a fur — mink or ermine — tail for the piggy's tail

4 buttons, or toothpaste-tube caps, or perfume-bottle caps, or soda-bottle caps for the feet

scraps of felt

felt-tipped marking pens

*how-to*

1. Wash out bleach bottle thoroughly, being sure to remove all traces of bleach; also remove the label.
2. Determine what you will use to cover the bottle: felt, other fabric, paint, or yarn. Cut out felt or fabric to fit (a piece

215

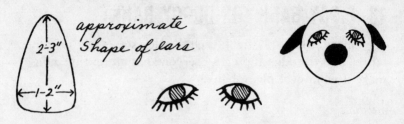

approximate *Shape of ears*

2-3"

←1-2"→

about 8" x 11" will fit the smaller bottles. Use strong fabric glue and press fabric in place. Or wind with yarn, gluing as you wind. Or simply spray — elegant gold, or a bright decorator color. (You can glue on sequins or dime-store "gems"; you can glue on fabric appliqués — tiny flowers or polka dots, perhaps); or glue on little buttons; or make a personalized piggy by writing the recipient's name with marking pen.

3. Trace around bottom of bottle and around cap on felt or fabric. Add 1½" to the diameter of the circle that will cover the cap; it can be the same color as the body, or a contrasting color. Glue these circles in place. (If you have sprayed color on, you can spray the bottom and the cap, too.)

4. Cut two ears from a contrasting color of felt; glue in place. Or draw the ears on with felt-tipped marking pen. Cut out felt eyes; or draw in with marking pens.

5. Cut out a slot in the piggy's top. Use a sharp single-edged razor, or a hobby knife.

6. Glue on button or bottle-top feet.

7. Glue on tail: twine, frayed at the ends; or cord with a knot at the end; or a pipe cleaner spiraled around a pencil; or a real fur tail; or a decorative tassel.

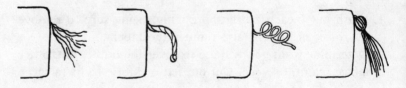

# 14. DUCK-Y PAJAMA BAG

An easy-to-concoct gift for children or teenagers is this pajama bag of felt. Make it in a favorite color, or to match a decorative scheme.

*materials*

felt: color A: 2 pieces 13″ x 18″
               2 pieces 5″ x 8″
    color B: 2 pieces 5″ x 5″
               2 pieces 2″ x 4″
1 yard grosgrain or velvet ribbon, 1″ to 2″ wide
1 button
cotton batting or old stockings for stuffing

*how-to*

1. Cut body: Place two 13″ x 18″ pieces of color A felt together; fold and cut as shown.
2. Cut legs: place the two 5″ square pieces of color B felt together; fold and cut as shown — the shape is a little like that of a hockey stick.
3. Sew around leg, topstitching ⅛″ from edge, and leaving top open. Repeat with other leg. Stuff both legs tightly to within ¾″ of top.

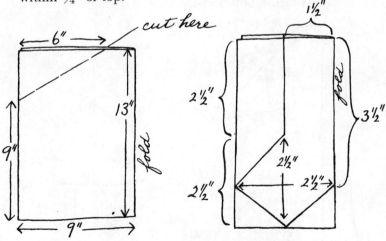

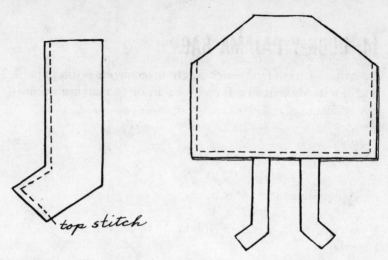

4. Pin legs to bottom of one piece of body as shown, feet pointing outward. Topstitch around body, down one side, across bottom, stitching legs firmly in place, and up other side.

5. Cut and sew head and neck: Place two pieces of felt, 5" x 8", color A, together, and cut as shown. Sew button eye in place on outside of one piece. Cut a 7" piece of ribbon, fold in half, turn in ends, and sew to outside of other head piece. Place both head pieces together and topstitch just around the head; stuff the head. Continue topstitching on both long sides of the neck, leaving the bottom open. Stuff the neck to ¾" from the bottom.

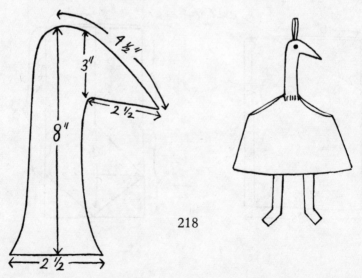

6. Pleat or gather both center sections of top of body until they are 3" wide. Pin neck of duck in place between both gathered sections. Stitch down firmly through all layers.
7. Make beak: Place both 2" x 4" pieces of color B felt together and cut in diamond shape as shown. Topstitch around two sides only as shown. Slip over point of duck's head. Use embroidery floss to attach beak from outside, making large back stitches.
8. Arrange remaining ribbon around duck's neck and tie with a four-in-hand tie or a bow. Stitch down invisibly to conceal stitches and keep tie in place.

*Note:* You can also make this duck in vinyl or upholstery fabrics: add ½" seam allowance to measurements where necessary; seam on wrong side and turn. This pattern also turns into a laundry bag, if a somewhat larger duck is made. Don't be afraid to work out your own design; sketch the pattern pieces on paper until you get the dimensions you want.

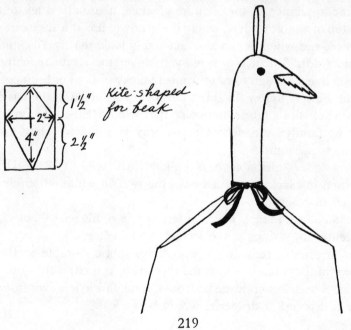

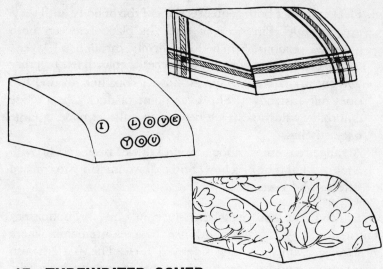

# 15. TYPEWRITER COVER

These days the typewriter has become almost as universal a home appliance as the vacuum cleaner; it usually is left out on top of a table or desk, where it is ready to use at a moment's notice, and where it can also constantly look unattractive and collect dust. But it is very easy to cover the useful machine attractively enough to suit the most finicky student or businessman. Simply follow the directions below for making the basic cover; choose a fabric and color that will appeal to the typist in the family; and decorate any way you choose. Here are some suggestions:

For a college girl, a cover of pink felt with "I LOVE YOU" written in black felt-tipped marking pen on white felt circles glued in place;

For a college man, a cover of felt in one of his school colors, accented by stripes in the second school color;

For anyone, a remnant of upholstery fabric suitable to the decor of the room in which the typewriter is used; if the home office is in a corner of the bedroom, some fabric left over from the bedspread or draperies would be perfect.

*materials*

½ yard felt or upholstery fabric

scraps of contrasting felt

*or* 1½ yards matching or contrasting corded tubing (optional)

*or* appliqués, buttons, braid, pompons, or any other trimmings
   that appeal to you

*how-to*

1. Cut one large piece and two matching side pieces from your
   fabric, following the pattern sketches.
2. Pin one side piece to one long edge of the larger piece from
   A to B as shown, with right sides together. Seam ½″ from
   edge. Repeat with other side piece and other long edge of
   large piece. Turn right side out.
3. Pin tubing along both seams; sew in place (optional). Or
   trim as suggested above, or any way you choose.

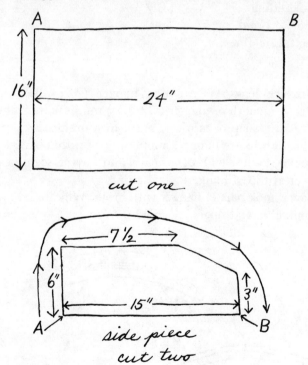

# 16. HANGER WITH ACCESSORY BAG

This project and the next are devoted to items for beautifying your closet and boudoir. You can use the same fabric and trimmings for all of them to make a matched set; or you can make them for yourself or as gifts as individual items.

This hanger comes with its own accessory bag attached, and is a very useful and unusual thing to have. A set of hangers, with or without the attached bag, can be made to match.

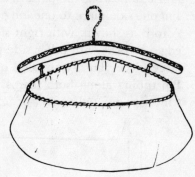

*materials*

1 wooden hanger
1 wire hanger
2 screw eyes
¾ yard any fabric
½ yard lining
2 yards 1″ braid
strong fabric glue

*how-to*

1. Measure length of wooden hanger (A to B); add 1″. Measure width of hanger (C to D); multiply by 2 and add 1″. Cut a strip of fabric to these measurements.
2. Glue fabric to hanger, molding it to shape with your fingers, folding ends over neatly and having seam of fabric meet at top of hanger.
3. Cover hook part of hanger with braid. Wind braid around, using glue and fingers to mold it to shape.

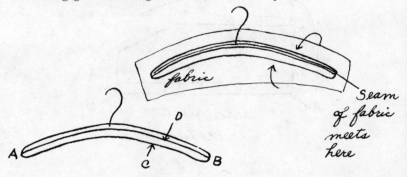

*fabric*

Seam of fabric meets here

4. Insert screw eyes about 3″ from end of hanger, underneath it as shown.
5. Remove hook part of wire hanger with wire cutter or pliers (or just bend it back and forth until it snaps). Pull down at center of straight part of hanger to make it into a sort of lopsided diamond shape.
6. Cut 18″ square pieces of fabric and lining. Place together with wrong sides facing and fold in half. Fold up bottom third as shown in sketch; and cut as shown in sketch.

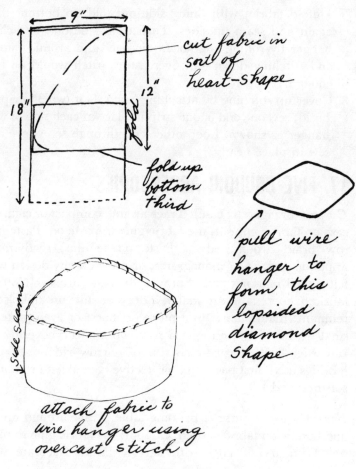

9″

18″

12″

fold

cut fabric in sort of heart-shape

fold up bottom third

pull wire hanger to form this lopsided diamond shape

Side seams

attach fabric to wire hanger using overcast stitch

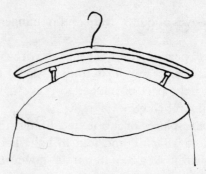

7. Unfold fabric; with lining side out fold up bottom third again and seam up sides. Turn right side out. Attach to hanger by rolling edge of fabric over and around hanger and stitching down — an overcasting stitch would be firm enough.
8. Cover up stitching by attaching braid. Cut two 3″ strips of braid; sew one end of one strip in place at each side of wire hanger as shown. Loop other end through screw eye and sew in place neatly.

# 17. FIVE BOUDOIR ACCESSORIES

*Compact* (or cigarette case): Trace around compact or cigarette case on fabric; cut out, use fabric glue to paste on. Paste narrow braid around edges. Paste on sequins, ready-made appliqué designs, or monograms; or draw on any design with felt-tipped marking pens. Spray with clear varnish. (Note on fabric: Choose fabric to match a dress or suit; use upholstery remnant; match fabric to a purse or shoes; or even paste on small scraps of fabric to get a patchwork effect, covering the raw edges with pasted-on strips of narrow ribbon. If thin fabric is used, first paste on a protective base of felt or another soft material.)

*Hand Mirror* for purse or dressing table: Trace around mirror and handle on fabric desired. Cut out; use fabric glue to paste on. Trim around edge with narrow braid. Decorate with artificial fabric flowers such as those used on millinery sequins, buttons, or odd earrings, glued on. Or use felt-tipped marking pens to draw in a doll's face, with rosy cheeks and perhaps "real" false eyelashes; edge the mirror with a yellow or black yarn "wig," glued on. Finish with clear varnish spray.

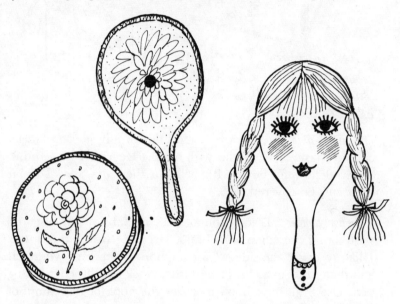

*Closet boxes:* Cover boxes in fabric to match other accessories. Simply trace around each side, bottom, top, and sides of top of box. Use any boxes: shoe boxes, hat boxes, candy boxes; they can be cardboard, plastic, or metal. To line box, trace around all sides and bottom of box on lining fabric. Glue lining and outer fabric in place. Cover corners, where fabric pieces meet, with narrow braid glued in place. Protect with a final spray of clear varnish. Make a set of boxes to match the hanger with its own accessory bag, above. I once made a nest of round boxes covered in white lace; stacked them together wedding-cake style and decorated the lid of the upper one with a wedding cake figure and tiny white flowers. It was a wonderful bridal shower centerpiece-and-gift combined.

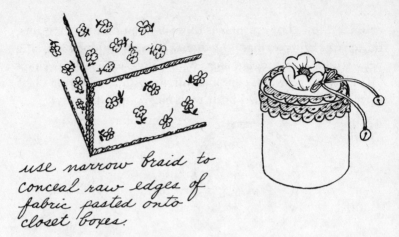

*use narrow braid to conceal raw edges of fabric pasted onto closet boxes.*

*Dressing-Table Jars:* Trace around lids of any jars on fabric; cut out, paste on. Edge lid with braid. Decorate with sequins, artificial flowers, bows with bells on their ties, etc. The jar itself can be covered, too.

*Camphor Holder:* Trace around sides on fabric; cut out and paste on. Trim edges with braid. Decorate with sequins, etc. I like to cover the sides of a camphor holder with white felt and then draw in a clock face with a black felt-tipped marking pen. Use braid or ribbon to cover the hook of the camphor holder, too.

There is really no limit to the variety of accessories that can be given this dress-up treatment. Clipboards and bulletin boards can be completely covered with fabric and edged with braid. Matchbooks, address books and calendars can be done

to match. Even an ordinary roller window shade can have decorative fabric pasted on with braid or other decorative trim added. Used frozen juice cans can be washed out; they can be spray-painted gold or any other color or covered with fabric; and their rims can be covered with adhesive-backed cloth tape that is available in dozens of colors, including gold and silver. Even clay flower pots can be glamorized to match your room: paste on fabric and trim; spray with clear varnish. This is an inexpensive but luxurious way to coordinate the hundred-and-one small accessories that would otherwise lurk hidden and unattractive in corners of drawers or closets.

## 18. CHRISTMAS TREE AND DECORATIONS

These pretty little trees never fail to attract attention in my shop window. They sell for at least $45 each; but they last and last for years and years. The secret is . . . velvet! What could be more elegant for a Christmas dinner centerpiece than a miniature tree of soft velvety shades of green. Extra pieces of velvet ribbon, scraps of braid and fringe, and other trimmings you've accumulated throughout the year, make the inexpensive Christmas decorations that can be miniature to go with the velvet tree or standard size for a real one.

*materials*

1 cone shape, 12" to 24" high (see step 1, below)
green or silver paint (spray or brush-on)
several yards of velvet ribbon, $\frac{5}{8}$" width; in one, two, or three
   shades of green; (yardage will vary according to size of
   tree; see step 1, below)
pins and/or fabric glue
12" square of green felt
3 or 4 jars tops
seed pearls or seed beads (optional)
dime-store "jewels," miniature tree decorations, odd earrings
   or buttons

1. Choose a styrofoam cone shape for your tree; or the heavy cardboard cone that string or twine come on; or take light-weight cardboard and roll to form a cone, using transparent tape and staples to hold cone together, and cutting off uneven bottom part of cone (a 12″ square of cardboard will make a cone 12″ high). You will need 8 to 10 yards of ribbon to cover a 12″ cone, 20 to 24 yards for an 18″ cone, and 30 to 36 yards for a 24″ cone.

2. If cone is of cardboard, trace around bottom of cone on an extra piece of cardboard; cut out. Use glue on bottom edge of cone to fasten cone to this base; use small strips of brown wrapping tape also if necessary.

3. Paint cone green or silver, using spray or brush-on paint.

4. Trace around bottom of cone on felt; cut out and glue on.

5. Glue three or more bottle or jar covers together to form the tree trunk. Or you might use an empty thread spool. Cover bottom and sides with green (or brown or black) felt. Trunk can be from 3″ to 5″ high.

6. Make loops and glue on to base. See basic instructions for making loops in Part VI. Cut several yard-long lengths of ribbon; cut into half-yard lengths. Fold each half-yard in four; cut to form four 4½″ lengths of ribbon. Glue on wrong side for about 1″ at each end. Attach both ends of strip side by side about 1½″ from bottom of cone, so that looped center hangs just below base of cone. Attach next loop, overlapping slightly. Continue attaching loops in a close row around base of cone. Then attach loops in a second row about ¾″ above base row, so that the looped centers of the second row overlap and come between looped centers of base row. Continue attaching loops in this way until you get near the top of the cone, alternating shades of green at random.

7. Use 3½″ lengths of ribbon to make the last two rows near the top. Overlap ends of loops very closely, molding glued ends with fingers. When dry, trim off excess.

8. Decorate tree: Attach some small, appropriate bauble at the very top. A glittering earring, button, paillette or fake "jewel" might do. Try a large gummed paper gold star; or a cardboard star brushed with glue and dipped into sequins or seed beads. If desired, scatter seed-bead decorations on your tree: put a drop of glue on the head of a pin and insert the pin into a tiny bead or pearl. Push point of pin through tree — right through velvet and into cone. (Note: pin-held decorations will work best on styrofoam or very heavy cardboard cone trees.) Or glue any other miniature decorations you choose directly onto velvet tree. (See below for Christmas bulb decorations.)
9. Glue tree trunk to base of cone.

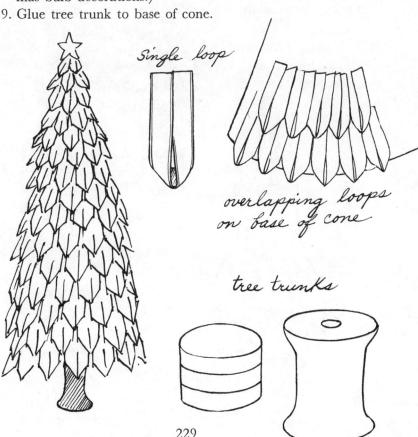

single loop

overlapping loops
on base of cone

tree trunks

229

*Christmas tree decorations:* Burned-out electric bulbs and scraps of velvet ribbon and other trimmings left over from a year's projects provide me with an annual supply of Christmas decorations. Use bulbs of every size and shape; the standard size bulbs are just right for real trees; but night-light bulbs make lovely miniature decorations. Paint the bulbs — gold, silver, or whatever you like. I spray a whole cluster of them at a time, usually with gold spray paint. Then, using fabric glue, paste the ends of a short length of narrow ribbon to the top of the bulb, leaving a loop at the top to hang the decoration from the tree. Use glue to attach braid or ribbon around the metal end of the bulb, covering the loop ends. Glue sequins, buttons or fake "jewels" on ribbon or on bulb.

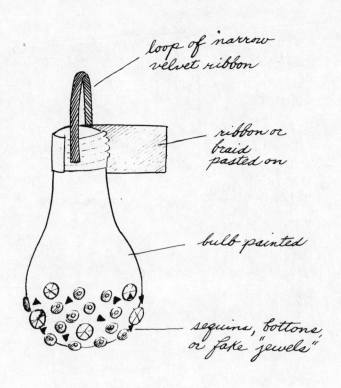

loop of narrow velvet ribbon

ribbon or braid pasted on

bulb painted

sequins, buttons or fake "jewels"

# VI

# From Appliqué to Zippers;
# A How-to Glossary

*Appliqué.* This is the application or attachment of a design cut out of one piece of fabric to a background of another fabric. Traditional appliqué work requires leaving a ¼″ allowance around the cut-out design; this is then turned under and laboriously blind stitched to the background fabric. But I have my own quick-and-easy system of appliqué. The cutouts are cut just as though they were paper dolls — right on the outline, with no ¼″ turn-under allowance. Then I simply use fabric glue to attach the cutouts wherever they should be. For additional support, and to create a more elaborate design, the pasted-on appliqués can then be given an embroidered outline by working small overcast stitching completely or part way around them.

Ready-made appliqué designs can be bought at notions counters — school emblems, monograms, flowers, chevrons, etc. It is easy to make your own: cut out any design — flower, boat, leaf, house — from a printed fabric; or draw your own pictures directly on fabric; or use a magazine or coloring-book picture as a design to transfer to fabric. Use felt-tipped marking pens to put an unfinished crossword puzzle or tic-tac-toe game on white felt or cotton; appliqué to garment.

¼ turnunder allowance

traditional appliqué designs

my watermelon appliqué
cut from a fruit-
design printed fabric,
pasted on, and partially
outlined with red and
green overcast stitching

*Buttons, fabric.* You can easily make fabric buttons to match anything by using your fabric and the button shapes to be found at the notions department; follow the directions on the package. I have an even faster trick: take a flat, shank-type button, turn it upside down on fabric and trace around it. Cut out; paste fabric to button. When dry, spray with clear varnish to prevent soiling and to keep edges from raveling.

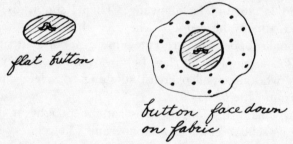

flat button

button face down
on fabric

*Camouflage.* Everything unsightly can be camouflaged. This includes stains, tears, uneven stitching, and the marks left when hems are let down. Appliqué will cover stains on and rips in fabric. Marking pens in the same color as the original fabric can blend in faded or stained areas; in contrasting colors, can draw designs over the discolored areas; and can even be used to "fake" embroidery. Old hemline marks that refuse to disappear can be hidden under rows of braid, rickrack, ribbon lace, or other trim; lines of uneven stitching can also be covered with these and, on the outer edges of a garment, by bias binding.

*Gluing fabric.* Use the strong white glues made especially for this purpose, on sale at notions counters and in upholstery supply shops. Put drops of glue at intervals around outside of the piece of fabric to be attached; put a few drops in center, too. Spread glue lightly, using a toothpick to smooth it into small areas. Press gently into place, using your fingers to stretch and mold the fabric and to press the outside edges down firmly. Work with fingers only, gently, a little bit at a time, and you will find the fabric is quite flexible while the glue is still damp. Then leave alone to dry, following time suggestions on the label; usually a few hours will do. Never use too much glue.

*Hems, adjustable.* To make one skirt do for two, evening length *and* dress length, is an easy matter. First, select a style for an evening skirt that is somewhat full, and as wide at the ankle as at the hip. Make it up, lined, in evening length, hem and all. (The Jiffy Skirt, Basic Style #4 in Part III, would be fine.) Buy snaps-by-the-yard (snap tape, which consists of two strips of twill fabric ribbon; one strip has snap heads set in it, and the other strip has the matching snap bottoms) in the length needed to go completely around the bottom of the skirt. Sew the snap-head twill strip around the inside of the skirt right at

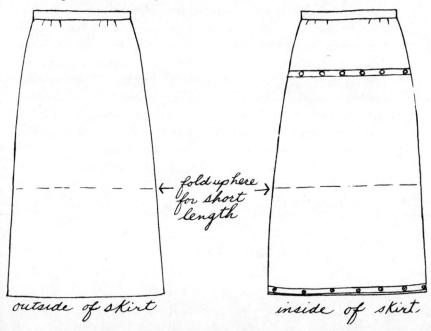

← fold up here → for short length

outside of skirt.                    inside of skirt.

the hem. Turn up the skirt inside to the desired short length; pin in place. Mark on the lining where the snap tape comes. Sew the other strip of snap tape in place on the inside lining. To wear the skirt short, snap the snaps. For evening, unsnap.

This trick works on coats, too. For a narrower slimmer look, make your evening skirt or coat in a sheath style, but slit the sides almost to the knee, Chinese style.

*Hooks and eyes.* Whether you are using the small metal hooks and eyes, or the large silk-covered ones, it is as important to sew them neatly as well as firmly. In fact, the neatest job is also the most secure. Choose hooks and eyes in a color as close to that of the fabric as possible. Use thread to match. Sew over and over, one stitch lying flat next to the other, as shown.

*Leather.* Leather is a fashionable trimming at any time, and an easy one to apply when you know how to work with it. I use regular thread and needle on my machine, but you may find it easier to work with heavy-duty thread and a heavier needle. Use large, but not basting, stitches. When sewing leather to fabric, place a strip of tissue paper over the leather, the fabric under the leather, and sew right through the paper. The paper pulls out easily afterward, and keeps your needle from catching. Use strips of leather instead of bias binding to pipe or edge a garment. Leather can also be glued in place. Use rubber cement for gluing leather to leather, as well as as leather to fabric.

234

*Needles.* Since you will be working with many different threads and fabrics, it is important to use the right needle for each job; but it is not necessary to keep a large number of needles on hand. Darning needles (or "sharps" as they are sometimes called) and embroidery needles come in assortments, so you get large- and small-eyed ones at the same time. There are also assortment packages of special needles, including the right equipment for hand sewing of upholstery-weight fabrics and of leather, and for use with yarn and other materials. Keep your needles sharp by pushing through an emery bag from time to time — this is the little strawberry-shaped piece often attached to tomato-shaped pin cushions.

For sewing-machine needles, follow the instructions that came with the machine.

*Patchwork.* In traditional patchwork, each small scrap was attached to its neighbors with ¼″ seams until large blocks, perhaps 12″ or 16″ square, were formed; then herringbone-stitch embroidery was worked over every little seam. Each block was seamed to another block, until a quilt of several dozen squares was formed; and once again herringbone stitches were worked over these seams. Lastly a backing of solid cotton fabric was put under the patchwork as a support.

Well, it was a good way to use up scraps of fabric, and a quilting bee was a pleasantly social way to spend an afternoon in good company, but . . .

Today we can appreciate the beautiful patchwork of an earlier day, and the effort that went into it. But we no longer have the long afternoons to spend trading scraps and endlessly matching patches. Here is my contemporary, quick-and-easy "recipe" for patchwork:

Start with the backing. A rectangle of cotton fabric about the size of a place mat will be a good foundation for a patch-work sampler, and when finished you can incorporate it into the Apron Skirt (Basic Style #3, Part III). Then get out your

235

ragbag. Any and every odd scrap you can lay your hands on will do — pieces left over from draperies and upholstery, from dresses and skirts, pieces cut off from hems, old dinner napkins, ribbons, discarded neckties. Use silk and velvet, cotton and corduroy, denim and damask. Contrasting textures add to the eye appeal. Take a few scraps and cut them into squares, rectangles, triangles, crescents, kite shapes; you want pieces having at least one dimension of about 3″ or 4″, although even long narrow strips can be used.

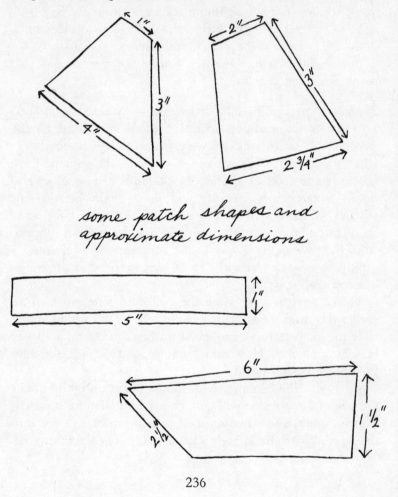

some patch shapes and approximate dimensions

Now take one of these patches, turn one of its straight edges under ¼" and pin anywhere at all on your backing, with wrong side of patch against wrong side of backing. Thread a needle—any color thread will do, but I prefer to use thread the same color as the backing fabric. Make a knot at the end and sew through the backing into the turned-under part of the patch only, so that your thread does not show on the right side of the patch. Use a combination stitch. Do not end off after you have stitched down one patch.

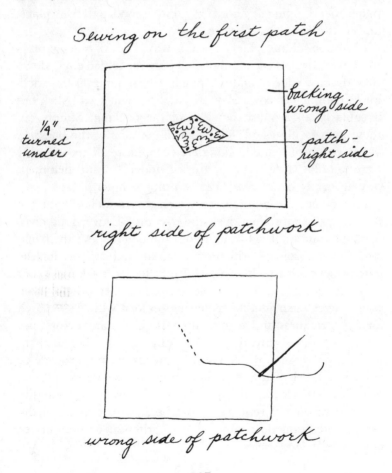

*Sewing on the first patch*

¼"
turned
under

backing
wrong side

patch-
right side

*right side of patchwork*

*wrong side of patchwork*

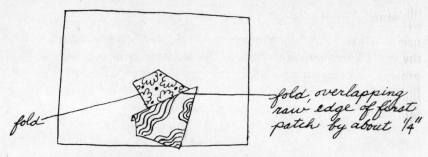

fold

fold, overlapping raw edge of first patch by about ¼"

Now take another patch, fold under ¼" on one side and place it so that the fold covers one of the raw edges of the first patch, overlapping it about ¼". Pin second patch in place, and sew to backing as before.

Continue adding patches in this way, folding one or sometimes two edges of each and sewing only the folded edges down over the raw edge of another patch. Continue until the backing is completely covered with patches, which will stick out irregularly all around the sides of the backing. Simply cut these uneven pieces off, following the outline of the backing. When patchwork and backing are even, baste all around near edge to hold. (Edges can be turned under ¼" and hemmed; or can simply be overcast, before using sampler.)

Last comes the embroidery which serves to highlight the patchwork. Embroider over the "seams" between patches, working your stitches through both the patches and the backing. The embroidery will provide additional support for the patchwork and attach it more firmly to the backing. Work herringbone, cross, buttonhole, or any other stitches you choose over each joining. Then embroider with each patch for extra richness and texture interest. Use many colors; use different types of thread; use many different stitches. If there is already a design on some of the patches, as in a brocade or a flocked fabric, outline it with embroidery. Work flowers, stars, wheels, leaves, vines on your patchwork. Repeat the same motif on different fabric patches, or on patches of the same fabric, using different colors. See stitch suggestions under *Stitches, embroidery*, below.

238

Wasn't that easy? You can do it in an evening. Now try making a garment of patchwork — use an old garment as the backing. See suggestions in Transformations #14 and 16 in Part IV.

*Plastics.* Any of the patterns in this book can be made out of the new shiny vinyl fabrics. Try a clear plastic tent or sleeveless coat. Try a vinyl shift or skirt. When you buy your plastic fabric, ask the salesman if there are any special sewing instructions for its use. Unless you have been given other instructions for your particular fabric choice, follow the directions given above for sewing on *leather*. Practice on a few scraps before you start on a garment of plastic, just to get the feel of it under your needle. You'll be delighted with the results.

*Pinning.* Do a lot of pinning, and you'll have very little basting and extra sewing to do. In general, pin at right angles to the direction of your stitches. Pin everything you can before you start to sew; remove pins as you sew. Keep a pin cushion or a box handy all the time.

*Pressing.* Do as little pressing as possible, only as much as is absolutely necessary. In general, use steam; work lightly; use a press cloth with wools and delicate fabrics; press in straight lines, never 'round and 'round; press darts from outside to inside, with fold of fabric facing down or toward center; and press seams from bottom to top, from hem to waist, from waist to shoulder. Try not to press hems: the sharply creased look is "out" and the soft fold is "in."

*Ribbon lace.* This is what I call the lace edging that is about 5/8″ wide, gently scalloped, and available in a wide range of colors. I use it instead of seam binding, to finish hems and seams and for hanger loops at waistbands. It makes a much prettier and more luxurious finish than the conventional rayon seam tape, and is well worth its slightly greater cost.

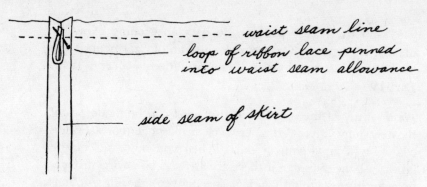

waist seam line

loop of ribbon lace pinned
into waist seam allowance

side seam of skirt

For hanger loops, cut two strips of ribbon lace about 6″ long. Fold each in half crosswise and pin cut ends together. Pin one loop of lace at each side of skirt, right at waistband, with cut ends of lace extending into waist seam allowance. When you finish waistband, simply stitch right through lace and remove pins.

To use as seam binding, hand or machine stitch straight edge of lace to edge of seam allowance; slip stitch scalloped edge of lace to lining.

To use as hem binding, hand or machine stitch straight edge of lace to edge of hem allowance; fold up hem and slip stitch or hem scalloped edge of lace to skirt or lining.

lining          lining

straight-edged
lace sewn to
seam allowance

scalloped
edge of lace
slip-stitched
to lining

lace as seam binding

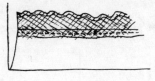

*lace as hem binding*

*Snaps.* Large silk-covered or small metal snaps will look best and hold best if sewn neatly as well as firmly. Choose snaps in a color as close to that of the fabric as possible (exception: silk-covered snaps can be chosen to contrast with fabric color). Use matching thread, and sew through holes, over and over, placing your stitches carefully one right next to the other, as shown,

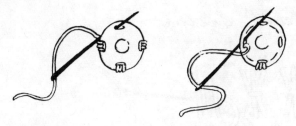

*Stitches, embroidery.* Although there are literally an infinite number of embroidery stitches, I find myself using the same ones over and over again. Alone and in combination, they do all sorts of things—enhance patchwork and appliqué, cover up stains and tears, and just add a pretty or whimsical touch wherever it might be needed.

*1. Stem Stitch (or Outline)*

241

## 2. Satin Stitch

## 3. Buttonhole Stitch

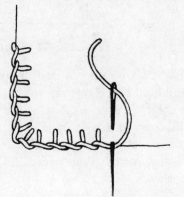

## 4. Sheath Stitch

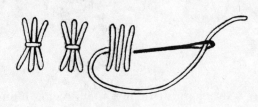

## 5. Cross Stitch

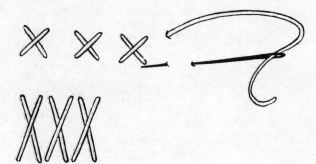

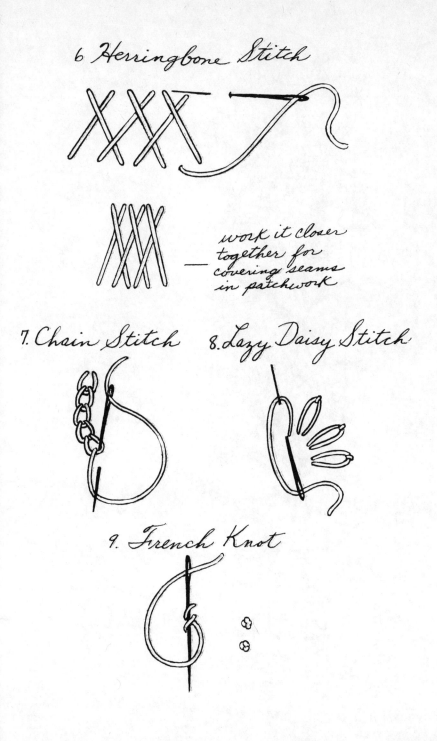

6 Herringbone Stitch

work it closer
together for
covering seams
in patchwork

7. Chain Stitch

8. Lazy Daisy Stitch

9. French Knot

orange stars

medium blue
herringbone-stitch
widely worked

yellow satin-stitch
flowers on green
stem-stitch vine

light blue herringbone-
stitch closely
worked

hot pink flowers
made up of
stem-stitch
rows worked
very close together

green stem-stitch
for stems and leaves

10. Some
Patchwork
Embroidery
Designs

pink
cross-stitch

dark red
wheel has
straight stitch
spokes and a
back-stitch rim

*Stitches, hand sewing.* Here are illustrations of some of the most useful ones:

1. *running stitch*

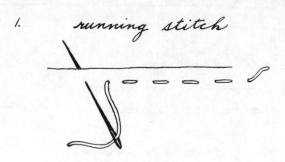

2. *back stitch*

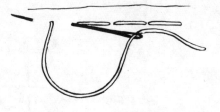

3. *combination stitch*
   *three running stitches and a backstitch*

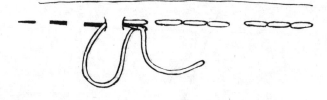

## 4. *basting*

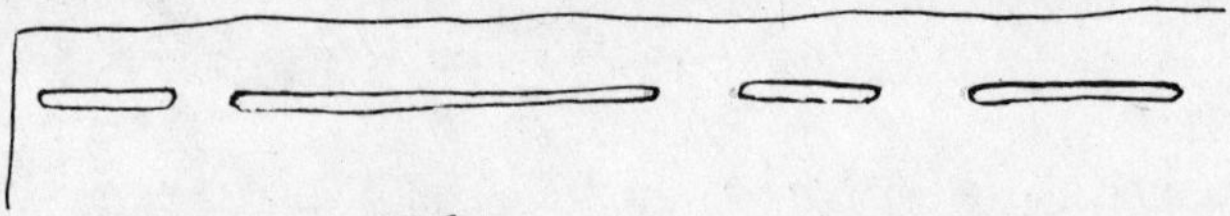

or

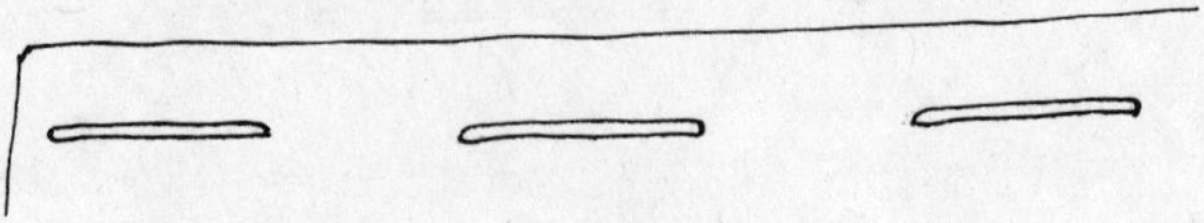

## 5. *overcasting*

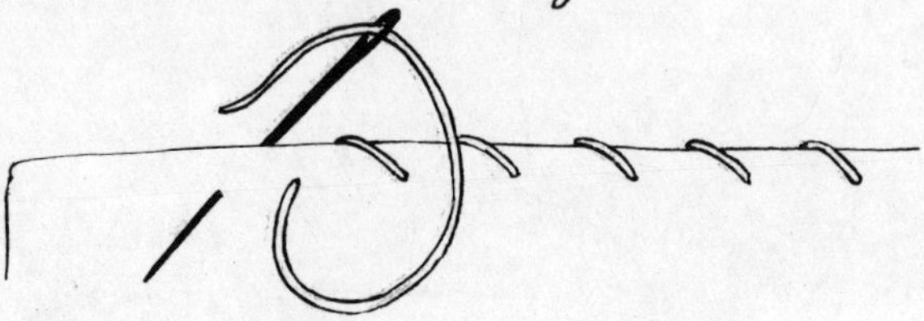

or

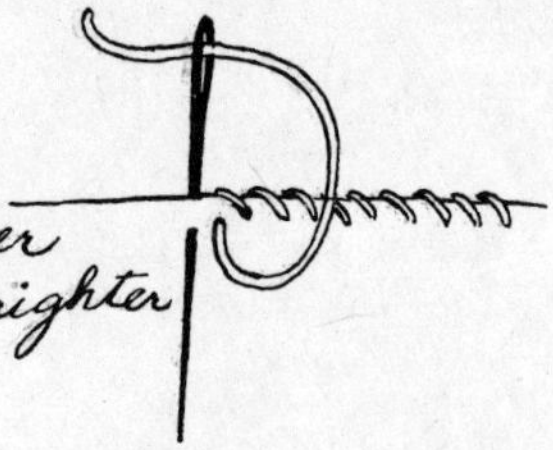

close together
needle held straighter
for applique

## 6. *hem or slip-stitch*

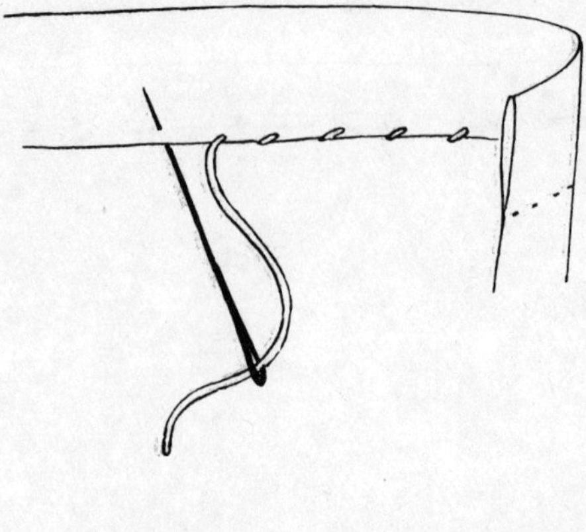

*Thread.* For nine sewing jobs out of ten, I use ordinary sewing thread, in a color to match the predominant color of the material. Heavier fabrics, such as denim, sailcloth, duck, and some upholstery materials, should be worked in heavy-duty thread.

For decorative stitchery, and I include even such things as sewing buttons, snaps, and hooks-and-eyes in this category, I prefer almost anything *except* ordinary sewing thread. Standard six-strand embroidery floss, in fine cotton or silk, is easy to keep on hand in a selection of colors. I like to use a different colored thread for each silk-covered snap sewn on a coat or jacket, for example. And when it comes to real embroidery, there is no limit to the different effects you can create by selecting your threads with imagination. Crocheting cotton, wool yarn, package cord, and metallic thread are only a few of the possibilities.

*Trimmings.* You will be able to attach such trimmings as braid neatly and invisibly by following these steps:
1) Pin trimming in place, allowing an extra ½" of trimming at beginning and end; turn under this extra bit and pin.
2) When trimming is to go around a corner neatly, make a mitered corner as shown.

right side

after sewing here
clip corner

wrong side
(clipping necessary for
bulky trimmings only

247

3) When trimming piece is too short and a new section must be added, simply overlap the cut ends of the old and new pieces about ½"; if you are working with the kind of braid that ravels, moisten the cut edges with a drop of fabric glue or turn under ½" on the top piece being joined.

4) To stitch invisibly, work from wrong side; use thread that matches trimming; use longer stitches on wrong side and catch into only one or two threads on right side of trimming.

*Velvet, antique.* Real antique velvet is very luxurious, and very, very expensive. I discovered that I can produce an antique finish on brand new velvet with the expenditure of only a little time and absolutely no extra money. Here's how.

Simply dip your length of velvet — whether it be yards of material or snips of ribbon — into lukewarm water. Work over the material with your fingers, crushing it gently until it is wet through. Lift material out of water, crush again to remove excess moisture, and lay flat over towels to dry. The crushing should have produced a soft all-over pattern of light and dark, as the nap of the velvet was pressed in different directions. If you think your material could still use more of this light-and-dark texturing, work it again with your fingers while it is still damp.

*Velvet loops.* These are the same velvet loops that were used to make the miniature Christmas tree (Accessory #18 in Part V). I use them for picture frames, too, and even hats; they are always original and lovely.

The ribbon can be of any width — ⅝", more, or even less. Cut into lengths of 4" to 6", depending on the width of the ribbon. For ⅝" ribbon, 4½" to 5" lengths are best. Place one strip of ribbon flat, nap side up, on a table in front of you. Put a few drops of glue on one side near end as shown. Keeping ribbon flat, bring one cut end up alongside of the other cut end. Overlap ends slightly so that they are glued together. Use fingers to adjust loop as shown. Use a few drops of glue to hold shape of loop.

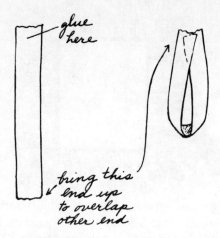

glue here

bring this end up to overlap other end

When attaching these loops to any base, such as the picture frame shown in the sketch, glue down one single row of loops first, having the loops cover the outside edge of the base. Then glue a second row of loops so that they cover the cut ends of the first row. Continue in this way until the base is entirely covered; the cut ends of the last row of loops will be at the inside edge. Here you can glue a narrow strip of matching braid or ribbon over them.

On a hat, the rows of loops will taper toward the center of the crown. The last row will end at that point, and its cut ends may be covered by a decorative button, a fabric flower, or a ribbon bow.

loops on a hat

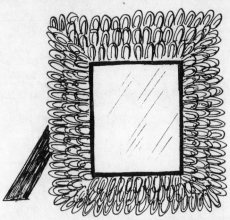

*Waistband closings:* There are many possibilities other than the customary button and buttonhole. I occasionally use two large silk-covered snaps, spaced about 1″ apart at the end of a waistband. This is easy, and it works satisfactorily for a loose-fitting waistband, perhaps one that is low enough to sit on the hips instead of at the waist proper. For a true-waist waistband I prefer to use hooks and eyes — the metal kind, since the large silk-covered ones are too bulky for a smooth fit. There are also special waistband hooks and eyes, which make the most secure and smooth closing. Remember to attach them firmly and attractively with neat, one-next-to-the-other stitches.

*Zippers.* Happily, zippers now can be found in almost every color under the sun; but I find I still occasionally have to dye them to match a particular fabric. Buy the right size for the job, and sew it in following the illustrated directions on the package. Easiest of all zippers to insert are the separating type, used for front closings on jackets and coats, and for back closings on blouses. Simply pin each side of the zipper in place on each side of the garment opening and stitch from bottom to top, with regular machine stitches or hand-sewn combination stitches. You can even use these, in the longest lengths, for skirts and shifts.

# Index

A-line dress, popover, 53
full-length, 53
A-line jumper, child's, 138–40
with drawstring neckline, 142–43
with pockets, 141
A-line skirt from straight skirt, 163–65
Accessories and gifts, 194–230
boudoir accessories, 224–27
Accessory bag, hanger with, 222–24
Address books, 226
Antique (heirloom) fabrics, 20–21
bonding, 26
reclaiming, 22–23
Antiquing velvet, 248
Apple cord-holder, 213
Appliqués, 38, 231. *See also* specific uses
Apron skirt, 62–66
Christmas motif, 69
full-length, 69
hobby motif, 68–69
hobo motif, 67
sewing motif, 68
Aprons,
cobbler, 78
many-pocketed, 192
At-home dress, popover, 52
Babies. *See* Children
Baby cap (for women), 146
Baby dress from man's or boy's shirt, 149–50
Bags. *See also* Handbags
accessory, hanger with, 222–24
duck-y pajama, 217–19
Bangles, 41
Bank, doggy or piggy, 215–16
Basket, sewing, 207–9
Bath skirt from bath towel, 171–72

Bath top from towels, 172–73
Beach tent coat, 102
Beads, 41
tweed, 203–4
Bean bag, ladybug, 212
Belts, 37
tape-measure, 206
Bias bindings, 39
Bibs,
clown, 211
ladybug, 210
strawberry, 211
Blouses,
bath top from hand towels, 172–73
dolman-sleeved, 54–56
pocket-edged, 58
reversible, 56–57
square-necked, 58
V-necked, 58
fringe-covered, 54–58
Mexican pants top from man's shirt, 152–53
popover, 47–52
smock-style (baby dress) from man's or boy's shirt, 149–50
Bonding fabric, 23–26
Bonnets,
Quaker sunbonnet, 128–32
infant's, 133
little girl's, 133
ruffled, for little girl, 144–46
Boudoir accessories, 224–27
camphor holder, 226
closet boxes, 225
compact or cigarette case, 224
dressing table jars, 226
hand mirror, 224–25
"Boutique," 10

251

Boxes, closet, 225
Boy's shirt, baby dress from, 149–50
Boy's sweater with built-in tie and collar, 147–49
Braid, 39
Buckles, 37
Bugles, 41
Bulletin boards, 226
Buttons,
  fabric-covered, 37, 232
  as trimmings, 40
Calendars, 226
Camouflage, 232
Camphor holder, 226
Cans, covered, 227
Cap, baby (for women), 146
Chef's hat, 134–37
Children, clothing and gifts for,
  bank, piggy or doggy, 215–16
  bean bag, ladybug, 212
  bibs, 210–11
    clown, 211
    ladybug, 210
    strawberry, 211
  bonnets, Quaker, 133
  bonnets, ruffled, 144–46
  dress, baby-style, from man's or boy's shirt, 149–50
  jumpers, A-line, 138–40
    with drawstring neckline, 142–43
    with pockets, 141
  pajama bag, duck-y, 217–19
  soakers for babies, 177–79
  sweater, boy's, with built-in tie and collar, 147–49
Christmas skirt, 62–63
  directions for, 69
Christmas tree and decorations, 227–30
Cigarette case, 224
Cleaning fabric, 21–22
Clipboards, 226
Closet boxes, 225
Clown bib, 211
Coats,
  jiffy, 124–25

jumper, 97–99
  beach tent, 102
  sheer fabric, 100–1
  sunny day, 184–86
  theater, 181–83
  wishbone, 92–94
  evening, 95
Cobbler shift, 74–77
  reversible, 78–79
Cobbler tunic or apron, 78
Compact, 224
Cord-holder apple, 213
Cowl-neck tent, sleeveless, 103–6
Crawford, Joan, 9, 10, 13
Curtain skirt, 189
Cutting, 44–46
Denim dress-ups, 186–88
Discotheque dress, 191
Doggy bank, 215–16
Dolman-sleeved blouse, 54–56
  pocket-edged, 58
  reversible, 56–57
  square-necked, 58
  V-necked, 58
Dolman-sleeved jacket, 59–61
Drapery weights, 38
Drawstring dress, 114
  lined, 114–16
  reversible, 117
Drawstring neckline, child's A-line jumper with, 142–43
Dresses. See also Jumpers
  baby-style, from boy's or man's shirt, 149–50
  cobbler shift, 74–77
    reversible, 78–79
  discotheque, 191
  drawstring, 114
    lined, 114–116
    reversible, 117
  fringe-covered, 154–58
  popover, 52
    A-line, 53
    at-home, 52
  sandwich-sign, 82–90
  the tent, 103–13
    front-closing, 111

252

lined, 112–13
    patch-pocketed, 109–10
    sleeveless cowl-neck, 103–6
    with sleeves, 107–8
Dressing-table jars, 227
Duck-y pajama bag, 217–19
Dungarees, denim dress-up, 186–87
Dyeing, 42
Earrings,
    gilded nut, 203
    safety pin, 202
    tweed, 202
Eggplant cord-holder, 213
Embroidery. *See also* specific uses
    re-embroidered skirt, 169–70
    stitches, 241
Evening wrap, jiffy, 126–27
Fabrics, 9–10
    bonding, 23–26
    care and handling of, 18–35
    cleaning, 21–22
    dyeing, 42
    finding, 19–21
    gluing, 233
    piecing, 26–32
    reclaiming, 22–23
    tips for experienced sewers, 32–35
Flower petal hat, 199–201
Flower pots, 227
Foundations, adding, 23–26
Fringe, 39
    reclaiming, 22
    skirt, blouse, or dress covered
        with, 154–58
Frogs, 38
Gifts and accessories, 194–230
Girls. *See* Children.
Glossary, 231–50
Glue, 42
Gluing fabric, 233
Half-and-half skirt, 166–67
Hand mirror, 224–25
Hand sewing stitches, 242
Handbags,
    little bag to match anything, 176–
        77
    lunchbox, 191

tote bag, 194–96
Hanger with accessory bag, 222–24
Hats,
    baby cap (for women), 146
    chef's, 134–37
    flower petal, 199–201
    pigtail, 192
Quaker sunbonnet, 128–32
    infant's, 133
    little girl's, 133
    ruffled bonnet for little girl, 144–
        46
Headbands, 198–99
Heirloom fabrics. *See* Antique
    fabrics
Hems. *See also* Skirts; etc.
    adjustable, 233–34
Hepburn, Audrey, 9, 10
Hobby skirt, 68–69
Hobo skirt, 67
Hooks and eyes, 234
    silk-covered, 37
Hot plate, 214
Infants. *See* Children
Interfacing, 41
Jackets,
    dolman-sleeved, 59–61
    jiffy, 118–23
    piecing, 26, 31
    redesigning, 27
Jars, dressing-table, 226
Jiffy coat, 124–25
Jiffy evening wrap, 126–27
Jiffy jacket, 118–23
Jiffy skirt, 70–71
    evening or at-home, 73
    lined, 73
    reversible, 72
Jumper coat, 97–99
    beach tent, 102
    sheer fabric, 100–1
Jumpers,
    child's A-line, 138–40
    with drawstring neckline, 142–
        43
    with pockets, 141
    wishbone, 96

253

Kennedy, Jacqueline, 9, 10
Lace, 39, 239–40
Ladybug bean bag, 212
Ladybug bib, 210
Leather, 234
Lining,
    bonding fabric, 23–26
    in piecing fabric, 27
    in reclaiming fabric, 23
Lunchbox handbag, 191
Man's at-home vest, 179–80
Man's shirt, baby dress from, 149–50
Man's shirt, Mexican pants top from, 152–53
Man's sweater with built-in collar and tie, 147–49
Many-pocketed aprons, 192
Matchbooks, 226
Mexican pants top from man's shirt, 152–53
Mirror, hand, 224–25
Mistakes, using, 16
Necklaces,
    tweed beads, 203–4
    twisted thread, 205
Needles, 235
Nightshirt from man's shirt, 152–53
Notions, 37
Nut earrings, gilded, 203
Paints, spray, 42
Pajama bag, duck-y, 217-19
Pants, party, from pettipants, 173–75
Pantskirt, 168–69
Party pants from pettipants, 173–75
Patch-pocketed tent, 109–10
Patches, iron-on, 39–40
Patchwork, 235–39
Patterns, using, 43–46
Pens, felt-tipped marking, 41
Petticoat, discotheque dress from, 191
Pettipants, party pants from, 173–75
Piecing fabric, 26–32
Piggy bank, 215–16
Pigtail hat, 192

Pins and pinnings, 42, 239
Plastics, 239
Pocket-edged blouse, 58
Popover blouse, 47–52
Popover dress, 52
    A-line, 53
    at-home, 52
Pressing, 239
Quaker sunbonnet, 128–32
    infant's, 133
    little girl's, 133
Reclaiming fabric, 22–23
Re-embroidered skirt, 169–70
Ribbon, 39
    in extending hem, 27
Ruffled bonnet, 144–46
Russell, Rosalind, 9, 10
Safety pin earrings, 202
Sandwich-sign dress, 82–90
Scarves, triangle, 196–97
Seam rippers, 42
Seams, ripping, 22
Sewing basket, 207–9
Sewing equipment, 42
Sewing motif on skirt, 68
Shawls, 23, 32–35
    jacket pieced from, 31
Shift, cobbler, 74–77
    reversible, 78–79
Shirt, man's (or boy's), baby dress from, 149–50
Shirt, man's, Mexican pants top from, 152–53
Shoebag, many-pocketed apron from, 192
Shoes to match anything, 190
Skirts,
    A-line, from straight skirt, 163–65
    apron, 62–66
        Christmas motif, 69
        full-length, 69
        hobby motif, 68–69
        hobo motif, 67
        sewing motif, 68
    bath, from bath towel, 171–72
    curtain, 189
    fringe-covered, 154–58

half-and-half, from two old skirts, 166–67
jiffy, 70–71
    evening or at-home, 73
    lined, 73
    reversible, 72
pantskirt from old skirt, 168–69
piecing, 26
redesigning, 27
re-embroidered, 169–70
tablecloth, 160–62
Sleeves,
    piecing, 26, 31
    redesigning, 27
Smock (baby dress) from man's or boy's shirt, 149–50
Snappers and eyelets, 37
Snaps, 241
    silk-covered, 37
Sneakers to match anything, 190
Soakers, baby's, 177–79
Sobo glue, 42
Stitches,
    embroidery, 241
    hand sewing, 242
Strawberry bib, 211
Sunbonnet, Quaker, 128–32
    infant's, 133
    little girl's, 133
Sunny day coat, 184–86
Sweater with built-in tie and collar, 147–49
Tablecloth skirt, 160–62
Tape-measure belt, 206
Taylor, Elizabeth, 9, 10, 62
Tent, the, 103–13

front-closing, 111
lined, 112–13
patch-pocketed, 109–10
sleeveless cowl-neck, 103–6
with sleeves, 107–8
Tent coat. *See* Jumper coat
Tent tunic, 102
Theater coat, 181–83
Thread, 247
Thrift shops, 20
Tote bag, 194–96
Towels,
    bath skirt from, 171–72
    bath top from, 172–73
Transformations, 147–92
Triangle scarves, 196–97
Trimmings, 39–40, 247–48
    finding, 19–20
    reclaiming, 22
Tunics,
    cobbler, 78
    tent, 102
Tweed beads, 203–4
Tweed earrings, 202
Twisted thread necklace, 205
Typewriter cover, 220–21
Velvet, antiquing, 248
Velvet loops, 248–49
Vest, man's at-home, 179–80
Waistband closings, 250
Washing fabrics, 21–22
Window shades, 226–27
Wishbone coat, 92–94
    evening, 95
Wishbone jumper, 96
Zippers, 250